pasta

100 everyday recipes

First published in 2011
LOVE FOOD is an imprint of Parragon Books Ltd

Parragon
Queen Street House
4 Queen Street
Bath BA1 1HE, UK

ISBN: 978-1-4454-3043-0

Printed in China

Produced by Ivy Contract
Photography by Charlie Paul

Notes for the Reader

This book uses both metric and imperial measurements. Follow the same units of measurement throughout; do not mix metric and imperial. All spoon measurements are level: teaspoons are assumed to be 5 ml, and tablespoons are assumed to be 15 ml. Unless otherwise stated, milk is assumed to be full fat, eggs and individual vegetables, such as potatoes, are medium, and pepper is freshly ground black pepper.

The times given are an approximate guide only. Preparation times differ according to the techniques used by different people and the cooking times may also vary from those given. Optional ingredients, variations or serving suggestions have not been included in the calculations.

Recipes using raw or very lightly cooked eggs should be avoided by infants, the elderly, pregnant women, convalescents and anyone suffering from an illness. Pregnant and breastfeeding women are advised to avoid eating peanuts and peanut products. Sufferers from nut allergies should be aware that some of the ready-made ingredients used in the recipes in this book may contain nuts. Always check the packaging before use. Vegetarians should be aware that some of the ready-made ingredients used in the recipes in this book may contain animal products. Always check the packaging before use.

pasta

introduction

Where would we be without pasta? It has to be the most useful invention ever in food – it is delicious, inexpensive, nutritious, quick and easy to cook, very satisfying and incredibly versatile. The fact that it comes in so many shapes and sizes makes it even more interesting, as well as fun to eat for adults and children alike.

The shape you use is largely a matter of choice, and you have about 200 different shapes to choose from! There are, of course, a few classic combinations. Spaghetti, for example, is the one to serve with meatballs or a rich, meaty, bolognese sauce – if you want to be both well fed and entertained, look out for the really long variety of spaghetti, which is quite a challenge to eat! Macaroni dishes simply wouldn't be the same made with any other shape of pasta, and Fettuccine Alfredo has a ring to the name that pasta lovers know well!

Pasta is almost foolproof to cook, but it's worth noting one or two points. Firstly, always bring the cooking water to a rapid boil before adding the pasta. Once the pasta is in the pan, adjust the heat so that the pasta cooks at a steady boil without boiling over. The most important thing to remember is not to overcook the pasta. 'Al dente' means 'still firm when bitten' and this is what you need to aim for when cooking pasta – eating limp, soggy pasta is quite an unpleasant experience. Follow the recommended cooking time in the recipe or on the packet and keep tasting toward the end of the time to make sure you get it just right – or you can, of course, follow the Italian tradition of throwing a test piece at the wall and if it sticks, you'll know it's done!

Making your own fresh pasta is surprisingly easy and there are a few recipes for you to try. For everyday use, though, fill your store cupboards with a good variety of pasta shapes, select your favourite dishes and make the most of this treasure of an ingredient.

soups & salads

minestrone

ingredients

serves 6

2 tbsp olive oil
55 g/2 oz rindless pancetta
    or lean bacon, diced
2 onions, sliced
2 garlic cloves, finely chopped
3 carrots, chopped
2 celery stalks, chopped
225 g/8 oz dried cannellini beans,
    soaked overnight in cold water
    to cover
400 g/14 oz canned chopped
    tomatoes
2 litres/64 fl oz beef stock
350 g/12 oz potatoes, diced
175 g/6 oz dried pepe bucato,
    macaroni or other soup
    pasta shapes
175 g/6 oz green beans, sliced
115 g/4 oz fresh or frozen peas
225 g/8 oz savoy cabbage,
    shredded
3 tbsp chopped fresh flat-leaf
    parsley
salt and pepper
fresh Parmesan cheese shavings,
    to serve

method

1 Heat the olive oil in a large, heavy-based saucepan.
Add the pancetta, onions and garlic and cook, stirring
occasionally, for 5 minutes.

2 Add the carrots and celery and cook, stirring
occasionally, for a further 5 minutes, or until all the
vegetables are softened.

3 Drain the soaked beans and add them to the pan with
the tomatoes and their can juices and the beef stock.
Bring to the boil, then reduce the heat, cover and
simmer for 1 hour.

4 Add the potatoes, re-cover, and cook for 15 minutes,
then add the pasta, green beans, peas, cabbage and
parsley. Cover and cook for a further 15 minutes, or
until all the vegetables are tender. Season with salt and
pepper. Ladle the soup into warmed soup bowls and
serve immediately with Parmesan cheese shavings.

hearty bean & pasta soup

ingredients

serves 4

4 tbsp olive oil
1 onion, finely chopped
1 celery stick, chopped
1 carrot, peeled and diced
1 bay leaf
1.2 litres/2 pints low-salt
    vegetable stock
400 g/14 oz canned chopped
    tomatoes
175 g/6 oz dried pasta shapes,
    such as farfalle, shells or twists
400 g/14 oz canned cannellini
    beans, drained and rinsed
200 g/7 oz spinach or chard, thick
    stalks removed and shredded
salt and pepper
40 g/1½ oz Parmesan cheese,
    finely grated, to serve

method

1 Heat the olive oil in a large heavy-based saucepan. Add the onion, celery and carrot and cook over a medium heat for 8–10 minutes, stirring occasionally, until the vegetables have softened. Add the bay leaf, stock and tomatoes, then bring to the boil.

2 Reduce the heat, cover and simmer for 15 minutes, or until the vegetables are just tender. Add the pasta and beans, then bring the soup back to the boil and cook for 10 minutes, or until the pasta is just tender. Stir occasionally to prevent the pasta sticking to the bottom of the pan and burning.

3 Season to taste, add the spinach and cook for a further 2 minutes, or until tender. Serve the soup in warmed bowls, sprinkled with Parmesan cheese.

variation

Try other beans, such as pinto, black-eyed beans or chickpeas, if you wish. Lentils, such as puy lentils, also make a tasty and nutritious alternative.

tomato broth with angel-hair pasta

ingredients

serves 4

500 g/1 lb 2 oz ripe tomatoes,
   peeled and halved
8 garlic cloves, peeled but
   left whole
1 Spanish onion, chopped
½ tsp saffron threads, lightly
   crushed
1 tsp sugar
1 bouquet garni
5-cm/2-inch strip thinly pared
   lemon rind
600 ml/1 pint vegetable
   or chicken stock
2 tbsp extra virgin olive oil
280 g/10 oz dried
   angel-hair pasta
salt and pepper

method

1 Put the tomatoes, garlic cloves, onion, saffron, sugar, bouquet garni and lemon rind into a large heavy-based saucepan. Pour in the stock and bring to the boil, then lower the heat, cover and simmer, stirring occasionally, for 25–30 minutes, until the tomatoes have disintegrated.

2 Remove the pan from the heat and leave to cool slightly. Remove and discard the garlic cloves, bouquet garni and lemon rind. Ladle the tomato mixture into a food processor or blender and process to a purée. Return the purée to the rinsed-out pan and season to taste with salt and pepper. Stir in the oil and bring to the boil. Add the pasta, bring back to the boil and cook for 2–4 minutes, until tender but still firm to the bite.

3 Taste and adjust the seasoning, if necessary. Ladle the broth and pasta into warmed soup bowls and serve immediately.

tortellini in broth

ingredients

serves 6

3 tbsp olive oil
1 red onion, finely chopped
2 garlic cloves, finely chopped
350 g/12 oz fresh beef mince
1 tsp finely chopped fresh thyme
1 fresh rosemary sprig,
    finely chopped
1 bay leaf
salt and pepper
1.7 litres/3 pints beef stock
400g/14 oz basic pasta dough
plain flour, for dusting
1 egg, lightly beaten

basic pasta dough

200 g/7 oz white bread flour
1 tsp salt
1 tbsp olive oil
2 eggs, lightly beaten

method

1 Heat the oil in a saucepan. Add the onion and garlic
   and cook over a low heat, stirring occasionally, until
   softened. Add the beef, increase the heat to medium
   and cook, stirring with a wooden spoon to break up
   the meat, for 8–10 minutes, until evenly browned.

2 Stir in the herbs, season to taste with salt and pepper,
   add 125 ml/4 fl oz of the stock and bring to the boil.
   Cover and simmer for 25 minutes, then remove the lid
   and cook until all the liquid has evaporated. Remove
   from the heat and discard the bay leaf.

3 Mix the pasta dough, working the oil and beaten eggs
   into the flour. Knead vigorously to form a stiff dough.
   Allow to rest, then roll out the dough thinly on a lightly
   floured surface. Using a plain biscuit cutter, stamp out
   rounds. Place the meat mixture in the centre of each
   round. Brush the edges with a little beaten egg, then
   fold them in half to make half moons and seal. Wrap
   these around the tip of your index finger until the
   corners meet and press together to seal. Place on a
   floured tea towel and leave to dry for 30 minutes.

4 Bring the remaining stock to the boil in a saucepan.
   Add the tortellini, bring back to the boil and cook until
   tender but still firm to the bite. Ladle the tortellini and
   broth into warmed soup bowls and serve immediately.

italian chicken soup

ingredients

serves 4

450 g/1 lb skinless, boneless
chicken breast, cut into
thin strips
1.25 litres/40 fl oz chicken stock
150 ml/5 fl oz double cream
115 g/4 oz dried vermicelli
salt and pepper
1 tbsp cornflour
3 tbsp milk
175 g/6 oz canned sweetcorn
kernels, drained

method

1 Place the chicken in a large saucepan and pour in the chicken stock and cream. Bring to the boil, then reduce the heat and simmer for 20 minutes.

2 Meanwhile, bring a large heavy-based saucepan of lightly salted water to the boil. Add the pasta, return to the boil and cook for 10–12 minutes, or until just tender but still firm to the bite. Drain the pasta well and keep warm.

3 Season the soup with salt and pepper. Mix the cornflour and milk together until a smooth paste forms, then stir it into the soup. Add the sweetcorn and pasta and heat through. Ladle the soup into warmed soup bowls and serve.

fish soup with anellini

ingredients

serves 6

2 tbsp olive oil
2 onions, sliced
1 garlic clove, finely chopped
1 litre/32 fl oz fish stock or water
400 g/14 oz canned chopped
    tomatoes
¼ tsp herbes de Provence
¼ tsp saffron threads
115 g/4 oz dried anellini
salt and pepper
450 g/1 lb monkfish fillet,
    cut into chunks
18 live mussels, scrubbed
    and debearded*
225 g/8 oz raw prawns, shelled
    and deveined, tails left on

* discard any damaged
mussels or any that do
not shut immediately
when tapped; once cooked
discard any mussels that
remain closed

method

1 Heat the olive oil in a large heavy-based saucepan.
Add the onions and garlic and cook over low heat,
stirring occasionally, for 5 minutes, or until the onions
have softened.

2 Add the fish stock with the tomatoes and their can
juices, herbs, saffron and pasta and season with salt
and pepper. Bring to the boil, then cover and simmer
for 15 minutes.

3 Add the fish, mussels and prawns. Re-cover the pan
and simmer for a further 5–10 minutes, until the
mussels have opened, the prawns have changed
colour, and the fish is opaque and flakes easily.
Ladle the soup into warmed bowls and serve.

white bean soup

ingredients

serves 4

175 g/6 oz dried cannellini beans,
    soaked overnight in cold
    water to cover
1.6 litres/48 fl oz chicken
    or vegetable stock
115 g/4 oz dried spirali
6 tbsp olive oil
2 garlic cloves, finely chopped
4 tbsp chopped fresh flat-leaf
    parsley
salt and pepper
fresh crusty bread, to serve

method

1 Drain the soaked beans and place them in a large, heavy-based saucepan. Add the stock and bring to the boil. Partially cover the pan, reduce the heat and simmer for 2 hours, or until tender.

2 Transfer about half the beans and a little of the stock to a food processor or blender and process to a smooth purée. Return the purée to the pan and stir well to mix. Return the soup to the boil.

3 Add the pasta to the soup, return to the boil and cook for 10 minutes, or until tender.

4 Meanwhile, heat 4 tablespoons of the olive oil in a small saucepan. Add the garlic and cook over low heat, stirring frequently, for 4–5 minutes, or until golden. Stir the garlic into the soup and add the parsley. Season with salt and pepper and ladle into warmed soup bowls. Drizzle with the remaining olive oil and serve immediately with crusty bread.

vegetable & bean soup

ingredients

serves 4–6

225 g/8 oz fresh broad beans
2 tbsp olive oil
2 large garlic cloves, crushed
1 large onion, finely chopped
1 celery stalk, finely chopped
1 carrot, peeled and chopped
175 g/6 oz new potatoes, diced
950 ml/30 fl oz vegetable stock
2 beefsteak tomatoes, peeled,
    deseeded and chopped
salt and pepper
1 large bunch of fresh basil,
    tied with kitchen string
200 g/7 oz courgette, diced
200 g/7 oz green beans, trimmed
    and chopped
55 g/2 oz dried vermicelli, in
    pieces, or small pasta shapes

pesto sauce

100 g/3½ oz fresh basil leaves
2 large garlic cloves
1½ tbsp pine nuts
50 ml/2 fl oz extra-virgin olive oil
55 g/2 oz finely grated
    Parmesan cheese

method

1 If the broad beans are very young and tender, they can be used as they are. If they are older, use a small, sharp knife to slit the skins, then 'pop' out the green beans.

2 Heat the olive oil in a large heavy-based saucepan, over medium heat. Add the garlic, onion, celery, and carrot and sauté until the onion is soft, but not brown. Add the potatoes, stock and tomatoes and season with salt and pepper. Bring the stock to the boil, skimming the surface if necessary, then add the basil. Reduce the heat and cover the pan. simmer for 15 minutes, or until the potatoes are tender.

3 Meanwhile, make the pesto sauce. Whiz the basil, garlic, and pine nuts in a food processor or blender until a thick paste forms. Add the extra-virgin olive oil and whiz again. Transfer to a bowl and stir in the cheese, then cover and chill until required.

4 When the potatoes are tender, stir the broad beans, courgette, green beans, and vermicelli into the soup and continue simmering until the vegetables are tender and the pasta is cooked. Adjust the seasoning if necessary. Remove and discard the bunch of basil.

5 Ladle the soup into bowls and add a spoonful of pesto sauce to each bowl.

chicken & chickpea soup

ingredients

serves 4

2 tbsp butter
3 spring onions, chopped
2 garlic cloves, crushed
1 sprig of fresh marjoram,
    finely chopped
350 g/12 oz chicken breasts, diced
1.2 litres/2 pints chicken stock
350 g/12 oz canned chickpeas,
    drained and rinsed
1 bouquet garni
salt and white pepper
1 red pepper, diced
1 green pepper, diced
115 g/4 oz dried macaroni
croûtons, to garnish

method

1 Melt the butter in a large pan over a medium heat. Add the spring onions, garlic, marjoram and chicken and cook, stirring frequently, for 5 minutes.

2 Add the chicken stock, chickpeas and bouquet garni. Season to taste with salt and white pepper. Bring the soup to the boil over a medium heat. Reduce the heat and simmer for about 2 hours. Add the diced peppers and pasta to the pan, then simmer for a further 20 minutes.

3 Ladle the soup into warmed serving bowls and garnish with croûtons. Serve immediately.

pasta niçoise

ingredients

serves 4

115 g/4 oz green beans, cut into
    2-inch/5-cm lengths
225 g/8 oz dried fusilli tricolore
100 ml/3½ fl oz olive oil
2 tuna steaks, about
    350 g/12 oz each
salt and pepper
6 cherry tomatoes, halved
55 g/2 oz black olives,
    pitted and halved
6 canned anchovies,
    drained and chopped
3 tbsp chopped fresh
    flat-leaf parsley
2 tbsp lemon juice
8–10 radicchio leaves

method

1 Bring a large, heavy-based saucepan of lightly salted water to the boil. Add the green beans, reduce the heat, and cook for 5–6 minutes. Remove with a slotted spoon and refresh in a bowl of cold water. Drain well. Add the pasta to the same pan, return to the boil, and cook for 8–10 minutes, or until tender but still firm to the bite.

2 Meanwhile, brush a griddle pan with some of the olive oil and heat until smoking. Season the tuna with salt and pepper and brush both sides with some of the remaining olive oil. Cook over medium heat for 2 minutes on each side, or until cooked to your liking, then remove from the griddle pan and reserve.

3 Drain the pasta well and tip it into a bowl. Add the green beans, cherry tomatoes, olives, anchovies, parsley, lemon juice, and remaining olive oil and season with salt and pepper. Toss well and let cool. Remove and discard any skin from the tuna and slice thickly.

4 Gently mix the tuna into the pasta salad. Line a large salad bowl with the radicchio leaves, spoon in the salad, and serve.

tuna & herbed fusilli salad

ingredients

serves 4

200 g/7 oz dried fusilli
1 red pepper, deseeded
    and cut into quarters
150 g/5½ oz asparagus spears
1 red onion, sliced
4 tomatoes, sliced
200 g/7 oz canned tuna in brine,
    drained and flaked

dressing

6 tbsp basil-flavoured oil or
    extra-virgin olive oil
3 tbsp white wine vinegar
1 tbsp lime juice
1 tsp mustard
1 tsp honey
4 tbsp chopped fresh basil, plus
    extra sprigs to garnish

method

1 Bring a large pan of lightly salted water to the boil.
Add the pasta, return to the boil, and cook for 8–10
minutes until tender but still firm to the bite.

2 Meanwhile, put the pepper quarters under a preheated
hot grill and cook for 10–12 minutes until the skins
begin to blacken. Transfer to a plastic bag, seal and
set aside.

3 Bring a separate pan of water to the boil, add the
asparagus, and blanch for 4 minutes. Drain and plunge
into cold water, then drain again. Remove the pasta
from the heat, drain, and set aside to cool. Remove the
pepper quarters from the bag and peel off the skins.
Slice the pepper into strips.

4 To make the dressing, put all the dressing ingredients
in a large bowl and stir together well. Add the pasta,
pepper strips, asparagus, onion, tomatoes, and tuna.
Toss together gently, then divide among serving bowls.
Garnish with basil sprigs and serve.

orecchiette salad with pears & blue cheese

ingredients

serves 4

250 g/9 oz dried orecchiette
1 head of radicchio, torn into pieces
1 oak leaf lettuce, torn into pieces
2 pears
3 tbsp lemon juice
250 g/9 oz blue cheese, diced
55 g/2 oz chopped walnuts
4 tomatoes, cut into quarters
1 red onion, sliced
1 carrot, grated
8 fresh basil leaves
55 g/2 oz corn salad
4 tbsp olive oil
3 tbsp white wine vinegar
salt and pepper

method

1 Bring a large heavy-based saucepan of lightly salted water to the boil. Add the pasta, return to the boil, and cook for 8–10 minutes, or until tender but still firm to the bite. Drain, refresh in a bowl of cold water and drain again.

2 Place the radicchio and oak leaf lettuce leaves in a large bowl. Halve the pears, remove the cores, and dice the flesh. Toss the diced pear with 1 tablespoon of lemon juice in a small bowl to prevent discolouration. Top the salad with the blue cheese, walnuts, pears, pasta, tomatoes, onion slices, and grated carrot. Add the basil and corn salad.

3 Mix the remaining lemon juice and the olive oil and vinegar together in a measuring cup, then season with salt and pepper. Pour the dressing over the salad, toss, and serve immediately.

penne & apple salad

ingredients

serves 4

2 large lettuces
250 g/9 oz dried penne
1 tbsp olive oil
8 red apples, diced
juice of 4 lemons
1 head of celery, sliced
115 g/4 oz walnut halves
250 ml/9 fl oz fresh garlic
    mayonnaise
salt and pepper

method

1 Wash, drain and pat dry the lettuce leaves with kitchen paper. Transfer them to the refrigerator for 1 hour, or until crisp.

2 Meanwhile, bring a large saucepan of lightly salted water to the boil. Add the pasta and olive oil, bring back to the boil and cook for 8–10 minutes, or until tender but still firm to the bite. Drain the pasta and refresh under cold running water. Drain thoroughly and cool.

3 Core and dice the apples, place them in a bowl and sprinkle with the lemon juice to coat them thoroughly – this will prevent them from turning brown. Mix together the cold pasta, sliced celery, diced apples and walnut halves and toss the mixture in the garlic mayonnaise. Season to taste with salt and pepper.

4 Line a salad bowl with the lettuce leaves and spoon the pasta salad on top. Chill until required.

warm pasta salad

ingredients

serves 4

225 g/8 oz dried farfalle or other
   pasta shapes
6 pieces of sun-dried tomato
   in oil, drained and chopped
4 spring onions, chopped
55 g/2 oz rocket, shredded
½ cucumber, deseeded and diced
salt and pepper
2 tbsp freshly grated Parmesan
   cheese

dressing

4 tbsp olive oil
½ tsp caster sugar
1 tbsp white wine vinegar
1 tsp Dijon mustard
salt and pepper
4 fresh basil leaves, finely shredded

method

1 To make the dressing, whisk the olive oil, sugar, vinegar, and mustard together in a bowl. Season with salt and pepper, then stir in the basil.

2 Bring a large, heavy-based saucepan of lightly salted water to the boil. Add the pasta, return to the boil, and cook for 8–10 minutes, or until tender but still firm to the bite. Drain and transfer to a salad bowl. Add the dressing and toss well.

3 Add the chopped sun-dried tomatoes, spring onions, rocket, and cucumber, season with salt and pepper, and toss. Sprinkle with the Parmesan cheese and serve warm.

pasta salad with chargrilled peppers

ingredients

serves 4

1 red pepper
1 orange pepper
280 g/10 oz dried conchiglie
5 tbsp extra virgin olive oil
2 tbsp lemon juice
2 tbsp pesto
1 garlic clove, crushed
3 tbsp shredded fresh basil leaves
salt and pepper

method

1 Put the whole peppers on a baking sheet and place under a preheated grill, turning the peppers frequently, for 15 minutes, until charred all over. Remove with tongs and place in a bowl. Cover with crumpled kitchen paper and set aside.

2 Meanwhile, bring a large saucepan of lightly salted water to the boil. Add the pasta, bring back to the boil and cook for 8–10 minutes, until tender but still firm to the bite.

3 Combine the olive oil, lemon juice, pesto and garlic in a bowl, whisking well to mix. Drain the pasta, add it to the pesto mixture while still hot and toss well. Set aside.

4 When the peppers are cool enough to handle, peel off the skins, then cut open and remove the seeds. Chop the flesh coarsely and add to the pasta with the basil. Season to taste with salt and pepper and toss well. Serve at room temperature.

spicy sausage pasta salad

ingredients

serves 4

125g/4½ oz dried conchiglie
2 tbsp olive oil
1 medium onion, chopped
2 garlic cloves, crushed
1 small yellow pepper, deseeded
   and cut into matchsticks
175 g/6 oz spicy pork sausage,
   such as chorizo, Italian
   pepperoni or salami, skinned
   and sliced
2 tbsp red wine
1 tbsp red wine vinegar
mixed salad leaves
salt

method

1 Bring a pan of lightly salted water to the boil over a medium heat. Add the pasta, bring back to the boil and cook for 8–10 minutes, or until tender but still firm to the bite.

2 Heat the oil in a pan over a medium heat. Add the onion and fry until translucent. Stir in the garlic, yellow pepper and sliced sausage and cook for about 3–4 minutes, stirring once or twice.

3 Add the wine, vinegar and reserved pasta to the pan, stir to blend well and bring the mixture just to the boil over a medium heat.

4 Arrange the salad leaves on 4 large serving plates, spoon over the warm sausage and pasta mixture and serve immediately.

pasta salad with melon & prawns

ingredients

serves 6

225 g/8 oz dried green fusilli
5 tbsp extra virgin olive oil
450 g/1 lb cooked prawns
1 Charentais melon
1 Galia melon
1 tbsp red wine vinegar
1 tsp Dijon mustard
pinch of caster sugar
1 tbsp chopped fresh
    flat-leaf parsley
1 tbsp chopped fresh basil
salt and pepper
1 oakleaf or quattro stagioni
    lettuce, shredded
fresh basil leaves, to garnish

method

1 Bring a large pan of salted water to the boil. Add the pasta, bring back to the boil and cook for 8–10 minutes, or until tender but still firm to the bite. Drain, toss with 1 tablespoon of the olive oil and leave to cool.

2 Meanwhile, peel and devein the prawns, then place them in a large bowl. Halve both the melons and scoop out the seeds with a spoon. Using a melon baller or teaspoon, scoop out balls of the flesh and add them to the prawns.

3 Whisk together the remaining olive oil, the vinegar, mustard, sugar, parsley and chopped basil in a small bowl. Season to taste with salt and pepper. Add the cooled pasta to the prawn and melon mixture and toss lightly to mix, then pour in the dressing and toss again. Cover with clingfilm and chill in the refrigerator for 30 minutes.

4 Make a bed of shredded lettuce on a serving plate. Spoon the pasta salad on top, garnish with basil leaves and serve.

meat & poultry

spaghetti bolognese

ingredients

serves 4

2 tbsp olive oil
1 tbsp butter
1 small onion, finely chopped
1 carrot, finely chopped
1 celery stalk, finely chopped
50 g/1¾ oz mushrooms, diced
225 g/8 oz minced beef
75 g/2¾ oz unsmoked bacon or
    ham, diced
2 chicken livers, chopped
2 tbsp tomato purée
125 ml/4 fl oz dry white wine
salt and pepper
½ tsp freshly grated nutmeg
300 ml/10 fl oz chicken stock
125 ml/4 fl oz double cream
450 g/1 lb dried spaghetti
2 tbsp chopped fresh flat-leaf
    parsley, to garnish
freshly grated Parmesan cheese,
    to serve

method

1 Heat the olive oil and butter in a large saucepan over medium heat. Add the onion, carrot, celery and mushrooms to the pan, then cook until soft. Add the beef and bacon and cook until the beef is evenly browned.

2 Stir in the chicken livers and tomato purée and cook for 2–3 minutes. Pour in the wine and season with salt, pepper and the nutmeg. Add the stock. Bring to the boil, then cover and simmer gently over low heat for 1 hour. Stir in the cream and simmer, uncovered, until reduced.

3 Bring a large saucepan of lightly salted water to the boil. Add the pasta, return to the boil and cook until tender but still firm to the bite. Drain and transfer to a warmed serving dish.

4 Spoon the sauce over the pasta, garnish with parsley and serve with Parmesan cheese.

spaghetti & meatballs

ingredients

serves 2

2 thick slices white bread,
    crusts removed

2 tbsp olive oil

1 red onion, chopped

2 garlic cloves, finely chopped

400 g/14 oz canned chopped
    tomatoes

8 basil leaves

2 tbsp tomato purée

1 tsp sugar

salt and pepper

450 g/1 lb minced beef

2 eggs

1 tbsp chopped fresh parsley

1 tbsp chopped fresh basil

350 g/12 oz dried spaghetti

freshly grated Parmesan cheese,
    to serve

method

1 Place the bread in a shallow bowl and add just enough water to cover. Soak for 5 minutes, then drain and squeeze the bread to remove all the liquid.

2 Heat the oil in a saucepan, add the onion and half the garlic and cook over medium heat, stirring occasionally, for 5 minutes. Add the tomatoes with their juice, basil leaves, tomato purée and sugar and season with salt and pepper. Bring to the boil, reduce the heat and simmer, stirring occasionally, for 20 minutes until thickened and pulpy.

3 Mix the bread, beef, eggs, remaining herbs, garlic and 1/2 tsp of salt by hand in a large mixing bowl. Roll small pieces of the meat mixture into balls. Drop the meatballs into the tomato sauce, cover the pan and cook over medium heat for 30 minutes.

4 Meanwhile, cook the spaghetti in a saucepan of lightly salted boiling water for 10 minutes, or until tender but still firm to the bite. Drain well.

5 Transfer the spaghetti to a large shallow serving bowl. Arrange the meatballs and sauce on top. Sprinkle 2 tablespoons of freshly grated Parmesan cheese over the top and serve with more cheese in a bowl on the side.

spaghetti alla carbonara

ingredients

serves 4

450 g/1 lb dried spaghetti
1 tbsp olive oil
225 g/8 oz rindless pancetta
    or lean bacon, chopped
4 eggs
5 tbsp single cream
salt and pepper
4 tbsp freshly grated Parmesan
    cheese

method

1 Bring a large, heavy-based saucepan of lightly salted
   water to the boil. Add the pasta, return to the boil and
   cook for 8–10 minutes, or until tender but still firm to
   the bite.

2 Meanwhile, heat the olive oil in a heavy-based frying
   pan. Add the chopped pancetta and cook over
   medium heat, stirring frequently, for 8–10 minutes.

3 Beat the eggs with the cream in a small bowl and
   season with salt and pepper. Drain the pasta and return
   it to the saucepan. Tip in the contents of the frying
   pan, then add the egg mixture and half the Parmesan
   cheese. Stir well, then transfer to a warmed serving
   dish. Serve immediately, sprinkled with the remaining
   Parmesan cheese.

tagliatelle with a rich meat sauce

ingredients

serves 4

4 tbsp olive oil, plus extra
   for serving
85 g/3 oz pancetta or rindless
   lean bacon, diced
1 onion, chopped
1 garlic clove, chopped finely
1 carrot, chopped
1 celery stalk, chopped
225 g/8 oz minced steak
115 g/4 oz chicken livers, chopped
2 tbsp strained tomatoes
125 ml/4 fl oz dry white wine
250 ml/8 fl oz beef stock or water
1 tbsp chopped fresh oregano
1 bay leaf
salt and pepper
450 g/1 lb dried tagliatelle
freshly grated Parmesan cheese,
   to serve

method

1 Heat the olive oil in a large, heavy-bottom saucepan. Add the pancetta or bacon and cook over medium heat, stirring occasionally, for 3–5 minutes, until it is just turning brown. Add the onion, garlic, carrot and celery and cook, stirring occasionally, for a further 5 minutes.

2 Add the steak and cook over high heat, breaking up the meat with a wooden spoon, for 5 minutes, until browned. Stir in the chicken livers and cook, stirring occasionally, for a further 2–3 minutes. Add the strained tomatoes, wine, stock, oregano and bay leaf and season with salt and pepper. Bring to the boil, reduce the heat, cover and simmer for 30–35 minutes.

3 When the sauce is almost cooked, bring a large saucepan of lightly salted water to the boil. Add the pasta, bring back to the boil and cook for 8–10 minutes, until tender but still firm to the bite. Drain, transfer to a warmed serving dish, drizzle with a little olive oil and toss well.

4 Remove and discard the bay leaf from the sauce, then pour the sauce over the pasta, toss again and serve immediately with grated Parmesan cheese.

chilli pork with tagliatelle

ingredients

serves 4

450 g/1 lb dried tagliatelle
3 tbsp peanut oil
350 g/12 oz pork fillet,
    cut into thin strips
1 garlic clove, finely chopped
1 bunch of spring onions, sliced
1-inch/2.5-cm piece fresh
    ginger, grated
2 fresh Thai chillies, deseeded
    and finely chopped
1 red pepper, deseeded
    and cut into thin sticks
1 yellow pepper, deseeded and
    cut into thin sticks
3 courgettes cut into thin sticks
2 tbsp finely chopped peanuts
1 tsp ground cinnamon
1 tbsp oyster sauce
55 g/2 oz creamed coconut, grated
salt and pepper
2 tbsp chopped fresh coriander,
    to garnish

method

1 Bring a large, heavy-based saucepan of lightly salted water to the boil. Add the pasta, return to the boil and cook for 8–10 minutes, or until tender but still firm to the bite.

2 Meanwhile, heat the peanut oil in a preheated wok or large, heavy-based frying pan. Add the pork and stir-fry for 5 minutes. Add the garlic, spring onions, ginger and Thai chillies and stir-fry for 2 minutes.

3 Add the red and yellow peppers and the courgettes and stir-fry for 1 minute. Add the peanuts, cinnamon, oyster sauce and creamed coconut and stir-fry for a further 1 minute. Season with salt and pepper. Drain the pasta and transfer to a serving dish. Top with the chilli pork, sprinkle with the chopped coriander and serve.

saffron linguine

ingredients

serves 4

350 g/12 oz dried linguine
pinch of saffron threads
2 tbsp water
140 g/5 oz ham, cut into strips
175 ml/6 fl oz double cream
55 g/2 oz freshly grated
    Parmesan cheese
salt and pepper
2 egg yolks

method

1 Bring a large, heavy-based saucepan of lightly salted water to the boil. Add the pasta, return to the boil and cook for 8–10 minutes, or until tender but still firm to the bite.

2 Meanwhile, place the saffron in a separate heavy-based saucepan and add the water. Bring to the boil, then remove from the heat and let stand for 5 minutes.

3 Stir the ham, cream and grated Parmesan cheese into the saffron and return the pan to the heat. Season with salt and pepper and heat through gently, stirring constantly, until simmering. Remove the pan from the heat and beat in the egg yolks. Drain the pasta and transfer to a large, warmed serving dish. Add the saffron sauce, toss well and serve.

rigatoni with ham tomato & chilli sauce

ingredients

serves 4

1 tbsp olive oil
2 tbsp butter
1 onion, chopped finely
150 g/5½ oz ham, diced
2 garlic cloves, chopped finely
1 fresh red chilli, deseeded
    and finely chopped
800 g/1 lb 12 oz canned
    chopped tomatoes
salt and pepper
450 g/1 lb rigatoni or penne
2 tbsp fresh flat-leaf parsley
6 tbsp freshly grated Parmesan
    cheese

method

1 Put the olive oil and 1 tablespoon of the butter in a large saucepan over a medium–low heat. Add the onion and fry for 10 minutes until soft and golden. Add the ham and fry for five minutes until lightly browned. Stir in the garlic, chilli & tomatoes. Season with a little salt and pepper.

2 Bring to the boil and then simmer over a medium-low heat for 30–40 minutes until thickened.

3 Cook the pasta in plenty of boiling salted water until tender but still firm to the bite. Drain and transfer to a warmed serving dish.

4 Pour the sauce over the pasta. Add the parsley, Parmesan cheese and the remaining butter. Toss well to mix and serve immediately.

farfalle with gorgonzola & ham

ingredients

serves 4

225 ml/8 fl oz crème fraîche
225 g/8 oz chestnut mushrooms,
    quartered
salt and pepper
400 g/14 oz dried farfalle
85 g/3 oz Gorgonzola cheese,
    crumbled
1 tbsp chopped fresh
    flat-leaf parsley, plus extra
    sprigs to garnish
175 g/6 oz cooked ham, diced

method

1 Pour the crème fraîche into a saucepan, add the
mushrooms and season to taste with salt and pepper.
Bring to just below the boil, then lower the heat and
simmer very gently, stirring occasionally, for 8–10
minutes, until the cream has thickened.

2 Meanwhile, bring a large pan of lightly salted water to
the boil. Add the pasta, bring back to the boil and cook
for 8–10 minutes, until tender but still firm to the bite.

3 Remove the pan of mushrooms from the heat and stir
in the Gorgonzola cheese until it has melted. Return
the pan to a very low heat and stir in the chopped
parsley and ham.

4 Drain the pasta and add it to the sauce. Toss lightly,
then divide among individual warmed plates, garnish
with the sprigs of parsley and serve.

variation

For a special occasion, omit the cooked ham and replace
with 175 g/6 oz pancetta or streaky bacon, diced.

pepperoni pasta

ingredients

serves 4

3 tbsp olive oil
1 onion, chopped
1 red pepper, deseeded
    and diced
1 orange pepper, deseeded
    and diced
800 g/1 lb 12 oz canned
    chopped tomatoes
1 tbsp sun-dried tomato purée
1 tsp paprika
225 g/8 oz pepperoni, sliced
2 tbsp chopped fresh flat-leaf
    parsley, plus extra to garnish
salt and pepper
450 g/1 lb dried garganelli
mixed salad leaves and vine
    tomatoes, to serve

method

1 Heat 2 tablespoons of the olive oil in a large, heavy-based frying pan. Add the onion and cook over low heat, stirring occasionally, for 5 minutes, or until softened. Add the red and orange peppers, tomatoes and their can juices, sun-dried tomato purée and paprika to the pan and bring to the boil.

2 Add the pepperoni and parsley and season with salt and pepper. Stir well and bring to the boil, then reduce the heat and simmer for 10–15 minutes.

3 Meanwhile, bring a large, heavy-based saucepan of lightly salted water to the boil. Add the pasta, return to the boil and cook for 8–10 minutes, or until tender but still firm to the bite.

4 Drain well and transfer to a warmed serving dish. Add the remaining olive oil and toss. Add the sauce and toss again. Sprinkle with parsley and serve immediately with mixed salad leaves and vine tomatoes.

macaroni with sausage, pepperoncini & olives

ingredients

serves 4

1 tbsp olive oil

1 large onion, chopped finely

2 garlic cloves, minced

450 g/1 lb pork sausage, peeled and chopped coarsely

3 canned pepperoncini, or other hot red peppers, drained and sliced

400 g/14 oz canned chopped tomatoes

2 tsp dried oregano

125 ml/4 fl oz chicken stock or red wine

salt and pepper

450 g/1 lb dried macaroni

12–15 black olives, pitted and cut into quarters

75 g/2¼ oz freshly grated cheese, such as Cheddar or Gruyère

method

1 Heat the oil in a large frying pan over medium heat. Add the onion and fry for 5 minutes until soft. Add the garlic and fry for a few seconds until just beginning to colour. Add the sausage and fry until evenly browned.

2 Stir in the pepperoncini, tomatoes, oregano and stock. Season with salt and pepper. Bring to the boil, then simmer the mixture over medium heat for 10 minutes, stirring occasionally.

3 Cook the macaroni in plenty of boiling salted water until tender but still firm to the bite. Drain and transfer to a warmed serving dish.

4 Add the olives and half the cheese to the sauce, then stir until the cheese has melted. Pour the sauce over the pasta. Toss well to mix. Sprinkle with the remaining cheese and serve at once.

fusilli with bacon, eggs & mushrooms

ingredients

serves 6

1 tbsp olive oil
4 rashers streaky bacon or pancetta
115 g/4 oz mushrooms, sliced
225 g/8 oz dried fusilli
2 eggs, beaten
115 g/4 oz Cheddar or mozzarella
    cheese, cubed
salt and pepper
chopped fresh flat-leaf parsley,
    to garnish

method

1 Heat the oil in a frying pan over a medium heat. Add the bacon and fry until crisp. Remove with tongs, cut into small pieces and keep warm.

2 Fry the mushrooms in the pan with the bacon fat for 5–7 minutes until soft. Remove from the heat.

3 Cook the pasta in a pan of lightly salted boiling water for 8–10 minutes, or until tender but still firm to the bite. Stir the mushrooms, beaten eggs and the cheese cubes into the pasta. Season with pepper and toss until the eggs have coated the pasta and the cheese has melted.

4 Transfer to a warm serving dish. Sprinkle with the bacon pieces and parsley and serve at once.

chorizo & mushroom pasta

ingredients

serves 6

680 g/1 lb 8 oz dried vermicelli
125 ml/4 fl oz olive oil
2 garlic cloves
125 g/4½ oz chorizo, sliced
225 g/8 oz exotic mushrooms
3 fresh red chillies, chopped
salt and pepper
2 tbsp fresh Parmesan cheese
     shavings, for sprinkling
10 anchovy fillets, to garnish

method

1 Bring a large, heavy-based saucepan of lightly salted water to the boil. Add the vermicelli, return to the boil and cook for 8–10 minutes, or until just tender, but still firm to the bite. Drain the pasta thoroughly, then place on a large, warmed serving plate and keep warm.

2 Meanwhile, heat the olive oil in a frying pan. Add the garlic and cook for 1 minute. Add the chorizo and exotic mushrooms and cook for 4 minutes. Add the chopped chillies and cook for a further minute.

3 Pour the chorizo and exotic mushroom mixture over the vermicelli and season with salt and pepper. Sprinkle with fresh Parmesan cheese shavings, garnish with anchovy fillets and serve at once.

linguine with lamb & yellow pepper sauce

ingredients

serves 4

4 tbsp olive oil
280 g/10 oz boneless lamb, cubed
1 garlic clove, finely chopped
1 bay leaf
125 ml/4 fl oz dry white wine
salt and pepper
2 large yellow peppers, deseeded
    and diced
4 tomatoes, peeled and chopped
250 g/9 oz dried linguine

method

1 Heat half the olive oil in a large, heavy-based frying pan. Add the lamb and cook over medium heat, stirring frequently, until browned on all sides. Add the garlic and cook for a further minute. Add the bay leaf, pour in the wine and season with salt and pepper. Bring to the boil and cook for 5 minutes, or until reduced.

2 Stir in the remaining oil, peppers and tomatoes. Reduce the heat, cover the pan and simmer, stirring occasionally, for 45 minutes.

3 Meanwhile, bring a large, heavy-based saucepan of lightly salted water to the boil. Add the pasta, return to the boil and cook for 8–10 minutes, or until tender but still firm to the bite. Drain and transfer to a warmed serving dish. Remove and discard the bay leaf from the lamb sauce and spoon the sauce onto the pasta. Toss well and serve at once.

chicken with basil & pine nut pesto

ingredients

serves 4

2 tbsp vegetable oil
4 skinless, boneless
    chicken breasts
350 g/12 oz dried farfalle
salt and pepper
sprig of fresh basil, to garnish

pesto

100 g/3½ oz shredded
    fresh basil
125 ml/4 fl oz extra-virgin olive oil
3 tbsp pine nuts
3 garlic cloves, finely chopped
salt
55 g/2 oz freshly grated
    Parmesan cheese
2 tbsp freshly grated romano
    cheese

method

1 To make the pesto, place the basil, olive oil, pine nuts, garlic and a generous pinch of salt in a food processor or blender and process until smooth. Scrape the mixture into a bowl and stir in the cheeses.

2 Heat the vegetable oil in a frying pan over medium heat. Fry the chicken breasts, turning once, for 8–10 minutes, or until the juices are no longer pink. Cut into small cubes.

3 Cook the pasta in plenty of lightly salted boiling water until tender but still firm to the bite. Drain and transfer to a warmed serving dish. Add the chicken and pesto, then season with pepper. Toss well to mix. Garnish with a basil sprig and serve warm.

tagliatelle with creamy chicken & shiitake sauce

ingredients

serves 4

25 g/1 oz dried shiitake
    mushrooms
350 ml/12 fl oz hot water
1 tbsp olive oil
6 bacon slices, chopped
3 boneless, skinless chicken
    breasts, sliced into strips
115 g/4 oz fresh shiitake
    mushrooms, sliced
1 small onion, chopped finely
1 tsp fresh oregano or marjoram,
    chopped finely
275 ml/9 fl oz chicken stock
300 ml/10 fl oz double cream
salt and pepper
450 g/1 lb dried tagliatelle
55 g/2 oz freshly grated
    Parmesan cheese
chopped fresh flat-leaf parsley,
    to garnish

method

1 Put the dried mushrooms in a bowl with the hot water and soak for 30 minutes, or until softened. Remove, squeezing excess water back into the bowl. Strain the liquid in a fine-meshed sieve and reserve. Slice the soaked mushrooms, discarding the stems.

2 Heat the oil in a large frying pan over medium heat. Add the bacon and chicken, then stir-fry for about 3 minutes. Add the dried and fresh mushrooms, onion and oregano. Stir-fry for 5–7 minutes, or until soft. Pour in the stock and the mushroom liquid. Bring to the boil, stirring. Simmer for about 10 minutes, continuing to stir, until reduced. Add the cream and simmer for 5 minutes, stirring, until beginning to thicken. Season with salt and pepper. Remove the pan from the heat and set aside.

3 Cook the pasta until tender but still firm to the bite. Drain and transfer to a serving dish. Pour the sauce over the pasta. Add half the Parmesan cheese and mix. Sprinkle with parsley and serve with the remaining Parmesan cheese.

chicken with creamy penne

ingredients

serves 2

200 g/7 oz dried penne
salt
1 tbsp olive oil
2 skinless, boneless chicken breasts
4 tbsp dry white wine
115 g/4 oz frozen peas
5 tbsp double cream
4–5 tbsp chopped fresh parsley,
    to garnish

method

1 Bring a large saucepan of lightly salted water to the boil. Add the pasta, bring back to the boil and cook for about 8–10 minutes, until tender but still firm to the bite.

2 Meanwhile, heat the oil in a frying pan, add the chicken and cook over a medium heat for about 4 minutes on each side.

3 Pour in the wine and cook over a high heat until it has almost evaporated. Drain the pasta. Add the peas, cream and pasta to the frying pan and stir well. Cover and simmer for 2 minutes. Garnish with fresh parsley and serve.

italian chicken spirals

ingredients

serves 4

4 skinless, boneless chicken breasts
25 g/1 oz fresh basil leaves
15 g/½ oz hazelnuts
1 garlic clove, crushed
salt and pepper
250 g/9 oz dried wholewheat
    fusilli
2 sun-dried tomatoes or fresh
    tomatoes
1 tbsp lemon juice
1 tbsp olive oil
1 tbsp capers
55 g/2 oz black olives

method

1 Beat the chicken breasts with a rolling pin to flatten evenly. Place the basil and hazelnuts in a food processor and process until finely chopped. Mix with the garlic and salt and pepper to taste.

2 Bring a pan of lightly salted water to the boil and cook the pasta for 8–10 minutes, or until tender but still firm to the bite. Meanwhile, place the chicken parcels in a steamer or colander set over the pan, cover tightly, and steam for 10 minutes. Using a sharp knife, dice the tomatoes.

3 Drain the pasta and return to the pan with the lemon juice, oil, tomatoes, capers and olives. Heat through.

4 Pierce the chicken with a skewer to make sure that the juices run clear and not pink. Slice the chicken, arrange over the pasta and serve.

seafood

conchiglie with smoked salmon & soured cream

ingredients

serves 4

450 g/1 lb dried conchiglie
300 ml/10 fl oz soured cream
2 tsp Dijon mustard
4 large spring onions, sliced finely
225 g/8 oz smoked salmon,
    cut into bite-sized pieces
finely grated rind of ½ lemon
salt and pepper
2 tbsp snipped fresh chives,
    to garnish

method

1 Bring a large, heavy-based saucepan of lightly salted water to the boil. Add the pasta, return to the boil and cook for 8–10 minutes, or until tender but still firm to the bite. Drain and return to the pan.

2 Add the soured cream, mustard, spring onions, smoked salmon and lemon rind to the pasta. Stir over a low heat until heated through. Season to taste with pepper.

3 Transfer to a serving dish and garnish with the chives. Serve warm or at room temperature.

fettuccine with sole & monkfish

ingredients

serves 4

85 g/3 oz plain flour
salt and pepper
450 g/1 lb lemon sole fillets,
    skinned and cut into chunks
450 g/1 lb monkfish fillets, skinned
    and cut into chunks
85 g/3 oz unsalted butter
4 shallots, finely chopped
2 garlic cloves, crushed
1 carrot, diced
1 leek, finely chopped
300 ml/10 fl oz fish stock
300 ml/10 fl oz dry white wine
2 tsp anchovy essence
1 tbsp balsamic vinegar
450 g/1 lb dried fettuccine
chopped fresh flat-leaf parsley,
    to garnish

method

1 Season the flour with salt and pepper and spread out
2 tablespoons on a plate. Coat all the fish pieces with it,
shaking off the excess. Melt the butter in a heavy-based
saucepan or flameproof casserole. Add the fish, shallots,
garlic, carrot and leek, then cook over low heat, stirring
frequently, for 10 minutes. Sprinkle in the remaining
seasoned flour and cook, stirring constantly, for
1 minute.

2 Mix the fish stock, wine, anchovy essence and balsamic
vinegar together in a jug and gradually stir into the fish
mixture. Bring to the boil, stirring constantly, then
reduce the heat and simmer gently for 35 minutes.

3 Meanwhile, bring a large heavy-based saucepan of
lightly salted water to the boil. Add the pasta, return to
the boil and cook for 8–10 minutes, or until tender but
still firm to the bite. Drain and transfer to a warmed
serving dish. Spoon the fish mixture onto the pasta,
garnish with chopped parsley and serve immediately.

mafalde with fresh salmon

ingredients

serves 4

350 g/12 oz salmon fillet
fresh dill sprigs, plus extra
    to garnish
125 ml/8 fl oz dry white wine
salt and pepper
6 tomatoes, peeled and chopped
150 ml/5 fl oz double cream
350 g/12 oz dried mafalde,
    tagliatelle or fettuccine
115 g/4 oz cooked, shelled prawns

method

1 Place the salmon in a large, heavy-based frying pan. Add a few dill sprigs, pour in the wine and season with salt and pepper. Bring to the boil, then reduce the heat, cover and poach gently for 5 minutes, or until the flesh flakes easily. Remove with a spatula, reserving the cooking liquid, and cool slightly. Remove and discard the skin and any remaining small bones, then flake the flesh into large chunks.

2 Add the tomatoes and cream to the reserved liquid. Bring to the boil, then reduce the heat and simmer for 15 minutes, or until the sauce has thickened.

3 Meanwhile, bring a large, heavy-based saucepan of lightly salted water to the boil. Add the pasta, return to the boil and cook for 8–10 minutes, or until tender but still firm to the bite. Drain and transfer to a warmed serving dish.

4 Add the salmon and prawns to the tomato sauce and stir gently until coated. Spoon the sauce onto the pasta, toss lightly, then serve, garnished with dill sprigs.

linguine with smoked salmon & rocket

ingredients

serves 4

350 g/12 oz dried linguine
2 tbsp olive oil
1 garlic clove, finely chopped
115 g/4 oz smoked salmon,
      cut into thin strips
55 g/2 oz rocket
salt and pepper
4 lemon halves, to garnish

method

1 Bring a large, heavy-based saucepan of lightly salted
   water to the boil. Add the pasta, return to the boil and
   cook for 8–10 minutes, or until tender but still firm to
   the bite.

2 Just before the end of the cooking time, heat the olive
   oil in a heavy-based frying pan. Add the garlic and
   cook over low heat, stirring constantly, for 1 minute.
   Do not allow the garlic to brown or it will taste bitter.
   Add the salmon and rocket. Season with salt and
   pepper and cook, stirring constantly, for 1 minute.
   Remove the pan from the heat.

3 Drain the pasta and transfer to a warmed dish. Add
   the smoked salmon and rocket mixture, toss lightly
   and serve, garnished with lemon halves.

fusilli with monkfish & broccoli

ingredients

serves 4

115 g/4 oz head of broccoli,
    divided into florets
3 tbsp olive oil
350 g/12 oz monkfish fillet,
    skinned and cut into
    bite-size pieces
2 garlic cloves, crushed
salt and pepper
125 ml/4 fl oz dry white wine
225 ml/8 fl oz double cream
400 g/14 oz dried fusilli bucati
85 g/3 oz Gorgonzola cheese,
    diced

method

1 Divide the broccoli florets into tiny sprigs. Bring a
saucepan of lightly salted water to the boil, add the
broccoli and cook for 2 minutes. Drain and refresh
under cold running water.

2 Heat the olive oil in a large, heavy-based frying pan.
Add the monkfish and garlic and season with salt and
pepper. Cook, stirring frequently, for 5 minutes, or
until the fish is opaque. Pour in the white wine and
cream and cook, stirring occasionally, for 5 minutes,
or until the fish is cooked through and the sauce has
thickened. Stir in the broccoli sprigs.

3 Meanwhile, bring a large, heavy-based saucepan of
lightly salted water to the boil. Add the pasta, return
to the boil and cook for 8–10 minutes, or until tender
but still firm to the bite. Drain the pasta and tip it into
the pan with the fish, add the cheese and toss lightly.
Serve immediately.

linguine alla puttanesca

ingredients

serves 4

450 g/1 lb plum tomatoes
3 tbsp olive oil
2 garlic cloves, finely chopped
10 anchovy fillets, drained and
    chopped
140 g/5 oz black olives, pitted
    and chopped
1 tbsp capers, rinsed
pinch of cayenne pepper
400 g/14 oz dried linguine
salt
2 tbsp chopped fresh flat-leaf
    parsley, to garnish
crusty bread, to serve

method

1 Peel the tomatoes by cutting a cross in the bottom
of each and placing in a heatproof bowl. Cover with
boiling water and let stand for 35–45 seconds. Drain
and plunge into cold water, then the skins will slide
off easily. Deseed and chop the tomatoes.

2 Heat the olive oil in a heavy-based saucepan. Add the
garlic and cook over low heat, stirring frequently, for
2 minutes. Add the anchovies and mash them to a pulp
with a fork. Add the olives, capers and tomatoes and
season with cayenne pepper. Cover and simmer for
25 minutes.

3 Meanwhile, bring a saucepan of lightly salted water to
the boil. Add the pasta, return to the boil and cook for
8–10 minutes, or until tender but still firm to the bite.
Drain and transfer to a warmed serving dish.

4 Spoon the anchovy sauce into the dish and toss the
pasta, using 2 large forks. Garnish with the parsley and
serve immediately with crusty bread.

pasta with tuna, garlic, lemon, capers & olives

ingredients

serves 4

350 g/12 oz dried conchiglie
    or gnocchi
4 tbsp olive oil
4 tbsp butter
3 large garlic cloves, sliced thinly
200 g/7 oz canned tuna, drained
    and broken into chunks
2 tbsp lemon juice
1 tbsp capers, drained
10–12 black olives, pitted
    and sliced
2 tbsp chopped fresh
    flat-leaf parsley
mixed salad leaves, to serve

method

1 Cook the pasta or gnocchi in plenty of boiling salted water until tender but still firm to the bite. Drain and return to the saucepan.

2 Heat the olive oil and half the butter in a frying pan over medium–low heat. Add the garlic and cook for a few seconds until just beginning to colour. Reduce the heat to low. Add the tuna, lemon juice, capers and olives. Stir gently until all the ingredients are heated through.

3 Transfer the pasta or gnocchi to a warmed serving dish. Pour the tuna mixture over the pasta. Add the parsley and remaining butter. Toss well to mix, then serve immediately with mixed salad leaves.

spinach & anchovy pasta

ingredients

serves 4

900 g/2 lb fresh, young
    spinach leaves
400 g/14 oz dried fettuccine
5 tbsp olive oil
3 tbsp pine nuts
3 garlic cloves, crushed
8 canned anchovy fillets,
    drained and chopped

method

1 Trim off any tough spinach stalks. Rinse the spinach leaves under cold running water and place them in a large saucepan with only the water that is clinging to them after washing. Cover and cook over high heat, shaking the pan from time to time, until the spinach has wilted, but retains its colour. Drain well, set aside and keep warm.

2 Bring a large heavy-based saucepan of lightly salted water to the boil. Add the fettuccine, return to the boil and cook for 8–10 minutes, or until it is just tender but still firm to the bite.

3 Heat 4 tablespoons of the olive oil in a separate saucepan. Add the pine nuts and cook until golden. Remove the pine nuts from the pan and set aside.

4 Add the garlic to the pan and cook until golden. Add the anchovies and stir in the spinach. Cook, stirring, for 2–3 minutes, until heated through. Return the pine nuts to the pan.

5 Drain the fettuccine, toss in the remaining olive oil and transfer to a warmed serving dish. Spoon the anchovy and spinach sauce over the fettuccine, toss lightly and serve at once.

penne with squid & tomatoes

ingredients

serves 4

225 g/8 oz dried penne
350 g/12 oz prepared squid
6 tbsp olive oil
2 onions, sliced
225 ml/8 fl oz fish stock or
    chicken stock
150 ml/5 fl oz full-bodied red wine
400 g/14 oz canned chopped
    tomatoes
2 tbsp tomato purée
1 tbsp chopped fresh marjoram
1 bay leaf
salt and pepper
2 tbsp chopped fresh parsley,
    to garnish

method

1 Bring a large, heavy-based saucepan of lightly salted water to the boil. Add the pasta, return to the boil and cook for 3 minutes, then drain and reserve until required. With a sharp knife, cut the squid into strips.

2 Heat the olive oil in a large saucepan. Add the onions and cook over a low heat, stirring occasionally, for 5 minutes, or until softened. Add the squid and stock, bring to the boil and simmer for 3 minutes. Stir in the wine, chopped tomatoes and their can juices, tomato purée, marjoram and bay leaf. Season to taste with salt and pepper. Bring to the boil and cook for 5 minutes, or until slightly reduced.

3 Add the pasta, return to the boil and simmer for 8–10 minutes, or until tender but still firm to the bite. Remove and discard the bay leaf. Transfer to a warmed serving dish, garnish with the parsley and serve immediately.

tagliatelle with prawns & scallops

ingredients

serves 6

450 g/1 lb raw prawns
25 g/1 oz butter
2 shallots, finely chopped
225 ml/8 fl oz dry white vermouth
350 ml/12 fl oz water
450 g/1 lb dried tagliatelle
2 tbsp olive oil
450 g/1 lb prepared scallops
2 tbsp snipped fresh chives
salt and pepper

method

1 Peel and devein the prawns, reserving the shells. Melt the butter in a heavy-based frying pan. Add the shallots and cook over a low heat, stirring occasionally, for 5 minutes, or until softened. Add the prawn shells and cook, stirring constantly, for 1 minute. Pour in the vermouth and cook, stirring, for 1 minute. Add the water, bring to the boil, then reduce the heat and simmer for 10 minutes, or until the liquid has reduced by half. Remove the frying pan from the heat.

2 Bring a large, heavy-based saucepan of lightly salted water to the boil. Add the pasta, return to the boil and cook for 8–10 minutes, or until tender but still firm to the bite.

3 Meanwhile, heat the olive oil in a separate heavy-based frying pan. Add the scallops and prawns and cook, stirring frequently, for 2 minutes, or until the scallops are opaque and the prawns have changed colour. Strain the prawn-shell stock into the frying pan. Drain the pasta and add to the frying pan with the chives and season to taste with salt and pepper. Toss well over a low heat for 1 minute, then serve.

tagliatelle & mussels with white wine, garlic & parsley

ingredients

serves 4

2 kg/4 lb 8 oz mussels, scrubbed*
1 large onion, chopped
3 garlic cloves, minced
550 ml/18 fl oz dry white wine
1 bay leaf
2 sprigs of fresh thyme
5 tbsp chopped fresh flat-leaf
    parsley
1 tbsp chopped fresh rosemary
4 tbsp butter
salt and pepper
450 g/1 lb dried tagliatelle or other
    broad-ribboned pasta

* discard any damaged mussels
or any that do not shut immediately
when tapped; once cooked discard
any mussels that remain closed

method

1 Clean the mussels by scrubbing the shells and pulling out any beards that are attached. Rinse the mussels well, discarding any with broken shells or that remain open when tapped.

2 Put the onion, garlic, white wine, herbs and 2 tablespoons of the butter in a saucepan. Bring to the boil, then reduce the heat. Add the mussels, then season with salt and pepper. Cover and cook over medium heat for 3–4 minutes, shaking the pan, until the mussels open. Remove from the heat. Lift out the mussels with a perforated spoon, reserving the liquid. Remove most of the mussels from their shells, reserving a few in their shells to garnish.

3 Cook the pasta until tender but still firm to the bite, then drain it and divide it between 4 individual serving bowls. Spoon the mussels over the pasta. Strain the mussel liquid and return to the pan. Add the remaining butter and heat until melted. Pour over the pasta, garnish with the mussels in their shells and serve the dish immediately.

mixed shellfish with angel-hair pasta

ingredients

serves 4

85 g/3 oz prepared squid
1 tsp cornflour
1 tbsp water
1 egg white
4 prepared scallops, sliced
85 g/3 oz raw prawns, shelled
    and deveined
salt
350 g/12 oz angel-hair pasta
3 tbsp peanut oil
55 g/2 oz mangetout
1 tbsp dark soy sauce
1 tbsp dry sherry
½ tsp light brown sugar
2 spring onions, shredded

method

1 Open out the squid and, with a sharp knife, score the inside with criss-cross lines. Cut into small pieces, about 2-cm/¾-inch square. Place in a bowl and cover with boiling water. When the squares have curled up, drain and rinse in cold water. Mix the cornflour and water together in a small bowl until a smooth paste forms and stir in about half the egg white. Add the scallops and prawns and toss until well coated.

2 Bring a large heavy-based saucepan of lightly salted water to the boil. Add the pasta, return to the boil and cook for 5 minutes, or until tender but still firm to the bite.

3 Meanwhile, heat the oil in a preheated wok or heavy-based frying pan. Add the mangetout, squid, scallops and prawns and stir-fry for 2 minutes. Stir in the soy sauce, sherry, sugar and spring onions and cook, stirring, for 1 minute. Drain the pasta and divide it between 4 warmed plates. Top with the shellfish mixture and serve at once.

fettuccine with scallops in porcini & cream sauce

ingredients

serves 4

25 g/1 oz dried porcini mushrooms
550 ml/18 fl oz hot water
3 tbsp olive oil
3 tbsp butter
350 g/12 oz scallops, sliced
2 garlic cloves, chopped very finely
2 tbsp lemon juice
250 ml/9 fl oz double cream
salt and pepper
350 g/12 oz dried fettuccine
    or pappardelle
2 tbsp chopped fresh flat-leaf
    parsley, to serve

method

1 Put the porcini and hot water in a bowl and soak for 20 minutes. Strain the mushrooms, reserving the soaking water, and chop coarsely. Line a sieve with kitchen paper and strain the mushroom water into a bowl.

2 Heat the oil and butter in a large frying pan over medium heat. Add the scallops and cook for 2 minutes until just golden. Add the garlic and mushrooms and stir-fry for 1 minute.

3 Stir in the lemon juice, cream and 125ml/4 fl oz of the mushroom water. Bring to the boil, then simmer over medium heat for 2–3 minutes, stirring constantly, until the liquid is reduced by half. Season with salt and pepper. Remove from the heat.

4 Cook the pasta in plenty of boiling salted water until tender but still firm to the bite. Drain and transfer to a warmed serving dish. Briefly reheat the sauce and pour over the pasta. Sprinkle with the parsley and toss well to mix. Serve at once.

seafood pasta pockets

ingredients

serves 4

2 tbsp virgin olive oil
2 fresh red chillies, deseeded
    and finely chopped
4 garlic cloves, finely chopped
800 g/1 lb 12 oz canned tomatoes
225 ml/8 fl oz dry white wine
salt and pepper
350 g/12 oz dried spaghetti
2 tbsp butter
115 g/4 oz prepared raw squid, sliced
175 g/6 oz raw jumbo prawns
450 g/1 lb live mussels, scrubbed
    and debearded*
1 crab, about 1.5 kg/3 lb 5 oz,
    freshly cooked, all meat
    removed
3 tbsp coarsely chopped fresh
    flat-leaf parsley
1 tbsp shredded fresh basil leaves

* discard any damaged mussels or
any that do not shut immediately
when tapped; once cooked, discard
any mussels that remain closed

method

1 Heat 1 tablespoon of the olive oil in a large pan.
Add half the chillies and half the garlic and cook over
medium heat, stirring occasionally, for 2–3 minutes.
Add the tomatoes with their can juices and the wine.
Reduce the heat and simmer for about 1 hour. Strain
the sauce, season and set aside.

2 Bring a saucepan of salted water to the boil. Add the
pasta, return to the boil and cook for 10 minutes, until
tender but still firm to the bite.

3 Heat the remaining olive oil with the butter in a large,
heavy-based saucepan. Add the remaining chilli and
garlic and cook over low heat, stirring occasionally, for
5 minutes, or until softened. Add the squid, prawns and
mussels, cover the pan and cook over high heat for 4–5
minutes, or until the mussels have opened. Remove
the pan from the heat and stir in the crab meat. Drain
the pasta and add it to the seafood with the chilli and
tomato sauce, parsley, and basil, tossing well to coat.

4 Cut out 4 large squares of baking parchment. Divide
the mixture between them, placing it on one half. Fold
over the other half and turn in the edges securely to
seal. Transfer to a baking sheet and bake in a preheated
oven, 180°C/350°F/Gas Mark 5, for 10 minutes, or until
the pockets have puffed up. Serve at once.

springtime pasta

ingredients

serves 4

2 tbsp lemon juice

4 baby globe artichokes

7 tbsp olive oil

2 shallots, finely chopped

2 garlic cloves, finely chopped

2 tbsp chopped fresh flat-leaf parsley

2 tbsp chopped fresh mint

350 g/12 oz dried rigatoni or other tubular pasta

2 tbsp unsalted butter

12 large raw prawns, shelled and deveined

salt and pepper

method

1 Fill a large bowl with cold water and add the lemon juice. Prepare the artichokes one at a time. Cut off the stems and trim away any tough outer leaves. Cut across the tops of the leaves. Slice in half lengthways and remove the central fibrous chokes, then cut lengthways into slices 5 mm/¼ inch thick. Immediately place the slices in the bowl of acidulated water to prevent discolouration.

2 Heat 5 tablespoons of the olive oil in a heavy-based frying pan. Drain the artichoke slices and pat dry with kitchen paper. Add them to the pan with the shallots, garlic, parsley and mint and cook over low heat, stirring frequently, for 10–12 minutes, or until tender.

3 Meanwhile, bring a large saucepan of lightly salted water to the boil. Add the pasta, return to the boil and cook for 8–10 minutes, or until tender but still firm to the bite.

4 Melt the butter in a frying pan, cut the prawns in half and add them to the pan. Cook, stirring occasionally, for 2–3 minutes, or until the prawns have changed colour. Season with salt and pepper.

5 Drain the pasta and tip it into a bowl. Add the olive oil and toss well. Add the artichoke mixture and the prawns and toss again. Serve immediately.

spaghetti with prawns & garlic sauce

ingredients

serves 4

3 tbsp olive oil

3 tbsp butter

4 garlic cloves, finely chopped

2 tbsp finely diced red pepper

2 tbsp tomato purée

125 ml/4 fl oz dry white wine

450 g/1 lb spaghetti or tagliatelle

350 g/12 oz raw shelled prawns

125 ml/4 fl oz double cream

salt and pepper

3 tbsp chopped fresh flat-leaf
    parsley, to garnish

method

1 Heat the oil and butter in a saucepan over medium–low heat. Add the garlic and red pepper. Fry for a few seconds until the garlic is just beginning to colour. Stir in the tomato purée and wine. Cook for 10 minutes, stirring continuously.

2 Cook the spaghetti in plenty of boiling salted water until tender but still firm to the bite. Drain and return to the saucepan.

3 Add the prawns to the sauce and raise the heat to medium–high. Cook for 2 minutes, stirring, until the prawns turn pink. Reduce the heat and stir in the cream. Cook for 1 minute, stirring constantly, until thickened. Season with salt and pepper.

4 Transfer the spaghetti to a warmed serving dish and pour over the sauce. Sprinkle with the parsley. Toss well to mix and serve at once.

spaghetti with clams

ingredients

serves 4

1 kg/2 lb 4 oz live clams, scrubbed
    under cold running water*
175 ml/6 fl oz water
175 ml/6 fl oz dry white wine
350 g/12 oz dried spaghetti
5 tbsp olive oil
2 garlic cloves, finely chopped
4 tbsp chopped fresh flat-leaf
    parsley
salt and pepper

* discard any clams with broken
or damaged shells and any that
do not shut when sharply tapped;
once cooked discard any clams
that remain closed

method

1 Place the clams in a large, heavy-based saucepan, add the water and wine, cover and cook over high heat, shaking the pan occasionally, for 5 minutes, or until the shells have opened.

2 Remove the clams with a slotted spoon and cool slightly. Strain the cooking liquid, through a sieve lined with cheesecloth, into a small pan. Bring to the boil and cook until reduced by about half, then remove from the heat. Meanwhile, discard any clams that have not opened, remove the remainder from their shells and reserve until required.

3 Bring a large saucepan of lightly salted water to the boil. Add the pasta, return to the boil and cook for 8–10 minutes, or until tender but still firm to the bite.

4 Meanwhile, heat the olive oil in a large, heavy-based frying pan. Add the garlic and cook, stirring frequently, for 2 minutes. Add the parsley and the reduced clam cooking liquid and simmer gently.

5 Drain the pasta and add it to the frying pan with the clams. Season with salt and pepper and cook, stirring constantly, for 4 minutes, or until the pasta is coated and the clams have heated through. Transfer to a warmed serving dish and serve immediately.

spaghetti & shellfish

ingredients

serves 4

225 g/8 oz dried short-cut
   spaghetti, or long spaghetti
   broken into 15-cm/6-inch
   lengths
1 tbsp olive oil
300 ml/10 fl oz chicken stock
1 tsp lemon juice
1 small cauliflower, cut into florets
2 carrots, sliced thinly
125 g/4½ oz mangetout
55 g/2 oz butter
1 onion, sliced
225 g/8 oz courgettes, thinly sliced
1 garlic clove, chopped
350 g/12 oz frozen shelled
   prawns, thawed
salt and pepper
2 tbsp chopped fresh parsley
25 g/1 oz freshly grated
   Parmesan cheese
½ tsp paprika, to sprinkle
4 unshelled prawns, to garnish
   (optional)
crusty bread, to serve

method

1 Bring a large, heavy-based saucepan of lightly salted
water to the boil. Add the spaghetti, return to the boil
and cook for 8–10 minutes, or until tender but still firm
to the bite. Drain, then return to the pan and stir in the
olive oil. Cover and keep warm.

2 Bring the chicken stock and lemon juice to the boil.
Add the cauliflower and carrots and cook for 3–4
minutes, until they are tender. Remove with a slotted
spoon and set aside. Add the mangetout and cook for
1–2 minutes, until they start to soften. Remove and
add to the other vegetables. Reserve the stock for
future use.

3 Melt half of the butter in a frying pan over medium
heat and cook the onion and courgettes for 3 minutes.
Add the garlic and prawns and cook for a further 2–3
minutes, until thoroughly heated through.

4 Stir in the reserved vegetables and heat through.
Season with salt and pepper, then stir in the remaining
butter. Transfer the spaghetti to a warmed serving dish.
Pour on the sauce and parsley. Toss well using 2 forks,
until thoroughly coated. Sprinkle on the grated cheese
and paprika and garnish with unshelled prawns, if
using. Serve at once, with crusty bread.

vegetarian

tagliatelle with pesto

ingredients

serves 4

450 g/1 lb dried tagliatelle
salt
sprigs of fresh basil,
    to garnish

pesto

2 garlic cloves
25 g/1 oz pine kernels
salt
115 g/4 oz fresh basil leaves
125 ml/4 fl oz olive oil
55 g/2 oz freshly grated
    Parmesan cheese

method

1 To make the pesto, put the garlic, pine kernels and a large pinch of salt into a blender or food processor and process briefly. Add the basil leaves and process to a paste. With the motor still running, gradually add the oil. Scrape into a bowl and beat in the Parmesan cheese. Season to taste with salt.

2 Bring a large saucepan of lightly salted water to the boil. Add the pasta, return to the boil and cook for 8–10 minutes, or until tender but still firm to the bite. Drain well, return to the saucepan and toss with half the pesto, then divide between warmed serving dishes and top with the remaining pesto. Garnish with sprigs of basil and serve.

variation

Use red pesto instead of green pesto for something a bit different. To make the pesto put 125 g/4 1/2 oz sun-blush tomatoes, 2 crushed garlic cloves, 4 tablespoons of lightly toasted pine kernels and 150 ml/5 fl oz extra virgin olive oil into a food processor and blend to a coarse paste. Use as above.

paglia e fieno with garlic crumbs

ingredients

serves 4

350 g/12 oz fresh white
    breadcrumbs
4 tbsp finely chopped fresh
    flat-leaf parsley
1 tbsp chopped fresh chives
2 tbsp finely chopped fresh
    sweet marjoram
3 tbsp olive oil, plus extra to serve
3–4 garlic cloves, finely chopped
55 g/2 oz pine nuts
salt and pepper
450 g/1 lb fresh paglia e fieno
55 g/2 oz freshly grated romano
    cheese, to serve

method

1 Mix the breadcrumbs, parsley, chives and marjoram together in a small bowl. Heat the olive oil in a large heavy-based frying pan. Add the breadcrumb mixture and the garlic and pine nuts, season with salt and pepper and cook over low heat, stirring constantly, for 5 minutes, or until the breadcrumbs become golden, but not crisp. Remove the pan from the heat and cover to keep warm.

2 Bring a large heavy-based saucepan of lightly salted water to the boil. Add the pasta, return to the boil and cook for 4–5 minutes, or until tender but still firm to the bite.

3 Drain the pasta and transfer to a warmed serving dish. Drizzle with 2–3 tablespoons of olive oil and toss to mix. Add the garlic breadcrumbs and toss again. Serve immediately with the grated romano cheese.

fettuccine alfredo

ingredients

serves 4

25 g/1 oz butter
225 ml/7 fl oz double cream
450 g/1 lb fresh fettuccine
1 tbsp olive oil
90 g/3¼ oz freshly grated
    Parmesan cheese, plus extra
    to serve
pinch of freshly grated nutmeg
salt and pepper
fresh flat-leaf parsley sprigs,
    to garnish

method

1 Place the butter and 150 ml/5 fl oz of the cream in a large saucepan and bring the mixture to the boil over medium heat. Reduce the heat and simmer gently for about 1½ minutes, or until slightly thickened.

2 Meanwhile, bring a large saucepan of lightly salted water to the boil. Add the fettuccine and oil, return to the boil and cook for 2–3 minutes until tender but still firm to the bite. Drain the fettuccine, return it to the pan and pour the sauce over it. Return the pan to low heat and toss the fettuccine in the sauce until coated.

3 Add the remaining cream, the Parmesan cheese and nutmeg to the fettuccine mixture and season with salt and pepper. Toss thoroughly to coat while gently heating through.

4 Transfer the fettuccine mixture to a warmed serving plate and garnish with parsley sprigs. Serve the dish immediately, with extra grated Parmesan cheese.

fettuccine with ricotta

ingredients

serves 4

350 g/12 oz dried fettuccine
3 tbsp unsalted butter
2 tbsp chopped fresh flat-leaf
    parsley, plus extra leaves
    to garnish
225 g/8 oz ricotta cheese
225 g/8 oz ground almonds
150 ml/5 fl oz soured cream
2 tbsp extra-virgin olive oil
125 ml/4 fl oz hot vegetable stock
pinch of freshly grated nutmeg
salt and pepper
1 tbsp pine nuts

method

1 Bring a large heavy-based saucepan of lightly salted water to the boil. Add the pasta, return to the boil and cook for 8–10 minutes, or until tender but still firm to the bite. Drain well and return to the pan. Add the butter and chopped parsley and toss thoroughly to coat.

2 Mix the ricotta, ground almonds and soured cream together in a bowl. Gradually stir in the olive oil, followed by the hot chicken stock. Season with nutmeg and pepper.

3 Transfer the pasta to a warmed dish, pour over the sauce and toss. Sprinkle with pine nuts, garnish with parsley leaves and serve immediately.

fettuccine with garlic, tomatoes & olives

ingredients

serves 4

4 plum tomatoes, peeled, deseeded and chopped
4 garlic cloves, finely chopped
8 black olives, stoned and finely chopped
1 fresh red chilli, deseeded and finely chopped
2 tbsp chopped fresh flat-leaf parsley
2 tbsp extra virgin olive oil
1 tbsp lemon juice
salt and pepper
280 g/10 oz dried fettuccine

method

1 Place the tomatoes in a large, non-metallic sieve set over a bowl. Cover and set aside in the refrigerator for 30 minutes.

2 Combine the garlic, olives, chilli, parsley, oil and lemon juice in a separate bowl. Season to taste with salt and pepper. Cover and set aside in the refrigerator until required.

3 Add the tomatoes to the garlic mixture, discarding the drained juice.

4 Bring a large saucepan of lightly salted water to the boil. Add the fettuccine, return to the boil and cook for 8–10 minutes, or until tender but still firm to the bite. Drain, then tip into a serving bowl. Add the garlic and tomato mixture and toss well. Serve immediately.

spaghetti olio e aglio

ingredients

serves 4

450 g/1 lb dried spaghetti
125 ml/4 fl oz extra-virgin olive oil
3 garlic cloves, finely chopped
salt and pepper
3 tbsp chopped fresh flat-leaf
    parsley

method

1 Bring a large, heavy-based saucepan of lightly salted water to the boil. Add the spaghetti, return to the boil and cook for 8–10 minutes, or until tender but still firm to the bite.

2 Meanwhile, heat the olive oil in a heavy-based frying pan. Add the garlic and a pinch of salt and cook over low heat, stirring constantly, for 3–4 minutes, or until golden. Do not allow the garlic to brown or it will taste bitter. Remove the pan from the heat.

3 Drain the pasta and transfer to a warmed serving dish. Pour in the garlic-flavoured olive oil, then add the chopped parsley and season with salt and pepper. Toss well and serve immediately.

farfalle with cream & cheese

ingredients

serves 4

450 g/1 lb dried farfalle
2 tbsp unsalted butter
350 g/12 oz petits pois
200 ml/7 fl oz double cream
pinch of freshly grated nutmeg
salt and pepper
55 g/2 oz freshly grated Parmesan
    cheese, plus extra to serve
fresh flat-leaf parsley sprigs,
    to garnish
crusty bread, to serve

method

1 Bring a large saucepan of lightly salted water to the boil. Add the pasta, return to the boil and cook for 8–10 minutes, or until tender but still firm to the bite, then drain thoroughly.

2 Melt the butter in a large, heavy-based saucepan. Add the petits pois and cook for 2–3 minutes. Add 150 ml/5 fl oz of the cream and bring to the boil. Reduce the heat and simmer for 1 minute, or until the mixture is slightly thickened.

3 Add the drained pasta to the cream mixture. Place the pan over low heat and toss until the farfalle are thoroughly coated. Season with nutmeg, salt and pepper, then add the remaining cream and the grated Parmesan cheese. Toss again and transfer to individual serving bowls. Garnish with parsley sprigs and serve immediately with extra Parmesan cheese, for sprinkling, and crusty bread.

fettuccine with peppers & olives

ingredients

serves 4

100 ml/3½ fl oz olive oil
1 onion, finely chopped
200 g/7 oz black olives, stoned
    and coarsely chopped
400 g/14 oz canned chopped
    tomatoes, drained
2 red, yellow or orange peppers,
    deseeded and cut into
    thin strips
salt and pepper
350 g/12 oz dried fettuccine
freshly grated pecorino cheese,
    to serve

method

1 Heat the oil in a large, heavy-based saucepan. Add the onion and cook over a low heat, stirring occasionally, for 5 minutes, or until softened. Add the olives, tomatoes and peppers and season to taste with salt and pepper. Cover and simmer gently over a very low heat, stirring occasionally, for 35 minutes.

2 Meanwhile, bring a large, heavy-based saucepan of lightly salted water to the boil. Add the pasta, return to the boil and cook for 8–10 minutes, or until tender but still firm to the bite. Drain the pasta and transfer to a warmed serving dish.

3 Spoon the sauce onto the pasta and toss well. Sprinkle generously with the pecorino cheese and serve immediately.

pipe rigate with gorgonzola sauce

ingredients

serves 4

400 g/14 oz dried pipe rigate,
    rigatoni, or penne
2 tbsp unsalted butter
6 fresh sage leaves
200 g/7 oz Gorgonzola
    cheese, diced
175–225 ml/6–8 fl oz
    double cream
2 tbsp dry vermouth
salt and pepper

method

1 Bring a large heavy-based saucepan of lightly salted water to the boil. Add the pasta, return to the boil and cook for 8–10 minutes, until tender but still firm to the bite.

2 Meanwhile, melt the butter in a separate heavy-based saucepan. Add the sage leaves and cook, stirring gently, for 1 minute. Remove and reserve the sage leaves. Add the cheese and cook, stirring constantly, over low heat until it has melted. Gradually, stir in 175 ml//6 fl oz of the cream and the vermouth. Season with salt and pepper and cook, stirring, until thickened. Add more cream if the sauce seems too thick.

3 Drain the pasta well and transfer to a warmed serving dish. Add the Gorgonzola sauce, toss well to mix and serve at once, garnished with the reserved sage leaves.

pasta with green vegetables

ingredients

serves 4

225 g/8 oz dried gemelli or other
    pasta shapes
2 tbsp chopped fresh parsley
2 tbsp freshly grated Parmesan
    cheese

sauce

1 head of broccoli, cut into florets
2 courgettes, sliced
225 g/8 oz asparagus, trimmed
125 g/4½ oz mangetout
125 g/4½ oz frozen peas
25 g/1 oz butter
3 tbsp vegetable stock
5 tbsp double cream
salt and pepper
large pinch of freshly grated
    nutmeg

method

1 Bring a large, heavy-based saucepan of lightly salted water to the boil. Add the pasta, return to the boil and cook for 8–10 minutes, or until tender but still firm to the bite. Drain the pasta, return to the pan, cover and keep warm.

2 Steam the broccoli, courgettes, asparagus and mangetout over a pan of boiling, salted water until just beginning to soften. Remove from the heat and plunge into cold water to prevent further cooking. Drain and reserve. Cook the peas in boiling, salted water for 3 minutes, then drain. Refresh in cold water and drain again.

3 Place the butter and vegetable stock in a saucepan over medium heat. Add all the vegetables except for the asparagus and toss carefully with a wooden spoon to heat through, taking care not to break them up. Stir in the cream, let the sauce heat through and season with salt, pepper and nutmeg.

4 Transfer the pasta to a warmed serving dish and stir in the chopped parsley. Spoon the sauce over and sprinkle on the freshly grated Parmesan cheese. Arrange the asparagus in a pattern on top. Serve immediately.

spaghetti alla norma

ingredients

serves 4

175 ml/6 fl oz olive oil
500 g/1 lb 2 oz plum tomatoes,
　　peeled and chopped
1 garlic clove, chopped
salt and pepper
350 g/12 oz aubergines, diced
400 g/14 oz dried spaghetti
½ bunch fresh basil, torn
115 g/4 oz freshly grated
　　pecorino cheese

method

1 Heat 4 tablespoons of the oil in a large saucepan.
Add the tomatoes and garlic, season to taste with salt
and pepper, cover and cook over a low heat, stirring
occasionally, for 25 minutes.

2 Meanwhile, heat the remaining oil in a heavy-based
frying pan. Add the aubergines and cook, stirring
occasionally, for 5 minutes, until evenly golden brown.
Remove with a perforated spoon and drain on
kitchen paper.

3 Bring a large pan of salted water to the boil. Add
the pasta, bring back to the boil and cook for 8–10
minutes, until tender but still firm to the bite.

4 Meanwhile, stir the drained aubergines into the pan of
tomatoes. Taste and adjust the seasoning, if necessary.

5 Drain the pasta and place in a warmed serving dish.
Add the tomato and aubergine mixture, basil and half
the pecorino cheese. Toss well, sprinkle with the
remaining pecorino cheese and serve immediately.

pappardelle with pumpkin sauce

ingredients

serves 4

55 g/2 oz butter
6 shallots, very finely chopped
salt
800 g/1 lb 12 oz pumpkin, peeled,
    deseeded and cut into pieces
pinch of freshly grated nutmeg
200 ml/7 fl oz single cream
4 tbsp freshly grated Parmesan
    cheese, plus extra to serve
2 tbsp chopped fresh
    flat-leaf parsley
350 g/12 oz dried pappardelle

method

1 Melt the butter in a large, heavy-based saucepan.
   Add the shallots, sprinkle with a little salt, cover and
   cook over a very low heat, stirring occasionally, for
   30 minutes.

2 Add the pumpkin pieces and season to taste with
   nutmeg. Cover and cook over a very low heat, stirring
   occasionally, for 40 minutes, or until the pumpkin is
   pulpy. Stir in the cream, Parmesan cheese and parsley
   and remove the saucepan from the heat.

3 Meanwhile, bring a large, heavy-based saucepan of
   lightly salted water to the boil. Add the pasta, return to
   the boil and cook for 8–10 minutes, or until tender but
   still firm to the bite. Drain, reserving 2–3 tablespoons
   of the cooking water.

4 Add the pasta to the pumpkin mixture and stir in the
   reserved cooking water if the mixture seems too thick.
   Cook, stirring, for 1 minute, then transfer to a warmed
   serving dish and serve immediately with extra grated
   Parmesan cheese.

tagliatelle with asparagus & gorgonzola sauce

ingredients

serves 4

450 g/1 lb asparagus tips
olive oil
salt and pepper
225 g/8 oz Gorgonzola, crumbled
175 ml/6 fl oz double cream
350 g/12 oz dried tagliatelle

method

1 Place the asparagus tips in a single layer in a shallow ovenproof dish. Sprinkle with a little olive oil and season with salt and pepper. Turn to coat in the oil and seasoning. Roast in a preheated oven, 230°C/450°F/Gas Mark 8, for 10–12 minutes, until slightly browned and just tender. Set aside and keep warm.

2 Combine the crumbled cheese with the cream in a bowl. Season with salt and pepper.

3 Cook the pasta in plenty of boiling salted water until tender but still firm to the bite. Drain and transfer to a warmed serving dish.

4 Immediately add the asparagus and the cheese mixture. Toss well until the cheese has melted and the pasta is coated with the sauce. Serve at once.

pasta with spiced leek, butternut squash & cherry tomatoes

ingredients

serves 4

150 g/5½ oz baby leeks, cut into
2-cm/¾-inch slices
175 g/6 oz butternut squash,
deseeded and cut into
2-cm/¾-inch chunks
1½ tbsp medium curry paste
1 tsp vegetable oil
175 g/6 oz cherry tomatoes
250 g/9 oz dried pasta shapes
2 tbsp chopped fresh coriander
leaves

white sauce

250 ml/9 fl oz skimmed milk
20 g/¾ oz cornflour
1 tsp mustard powder
1 small onion, left whole
2 small bay leaves
4 tsp grated Parmesan cheese

method

1 To make the white sauce, put the milk into a saucepan
with the cornflour, mustard, onion and bay leaves.
Whisk over medium heat until thick. Remove from the
heat, discard the onion and bay leaves and stir in the
cheese. Set aside, stirring occasionally to prevent a
skin forming.

2 Bring a large saucepan of water to the boil, add the
leeks and cook for 2 minutes. Add the butternut squash
and cook for a further 2 minutes. Drain in a colander.

3 Mix the curry paste with the oil in a large bowl.
Toss the leeks and butternut squash in the mixture
to coat thoroughly. Transfer the leeks and butternut
squash to a non-stick baking sheet and roast in a
preheated oven, 200°C/ 400°F/Gas Mark 6, for
10 minutes until golden brown. Add the tomatoes
and roast for a further 5 minutes.

4 Meanwhile, cook the pasta in a large pan according
to the instructions on the packet and drain.

5 Put the white sauce into a large saucepan and warm
over low heat. Add the leeks, butternut squash,
tomatoes and coriander and stir in the warm pasta.
Mix well and serve.

spaghetti with tomato, garlic & basil sauce

ingredients

serves 4

5 tbsp extra-virgin olive oil
1 onion, chopped finely
800 g/1 lb 12 oz canned chopped
    tomatoes
4 garlic cloves, cut into quarters
salt and pepper
450 g/1 lb dried spaghetti
large handful fresh basil leaves,
    shredded
fresh Parmesan cheese shavings,
    to serve

method

1 Heat the oil in a large saucepan over medium heat. Add the onion and fry gently for 5 minutes until soft. Add the tomatoes and garlic. Bring to the boil, then simmer over medium–low heat for 25–30 minutes until the oil separates from the tomato. Season with salt and pepper.

2 Cook the pasta in plenty of boiling salted water until tender but still firm to the bite. Drain and transfer to a warmed serving dish.

3 Pour the sauce over the pasta. Add the basil and toss well to mix. Serve with the Parmesan cheese shavings.

fusilli with herbed sun-dried tomato sauce

ingredients

serves 4

85 g/3 oz sun-dried tomatoes
  (not in oil)
750 ml/24 fl oz boiling water
2 tbsp olive oil
1 onion, chopped finely
2 large garlic cloves, sliced finely
2 tbsp chopped fresh flat-leaf
  parsley
2 tsp chopped fresh oregano
1 tsp chopped fresh rosemary
salt and pepper
350 g/12 oz dried fusilli
10 fresh basil leaves, shredded and
  3 tbsp freshly grated Parmesan
  cheese, to serve

method

1 Put the tomatoes and boiling water in a bowl and let stand for 5 minutes. Using a perforated spoon, remove one third of the tomatoes from the bowl. Cut into bite-size pieces. Put the remaining tomatoes and water into a blender and purée.

2 Heat the oil in a large frying pan over medium heat. Add the onion and gently fry for 5 minutes until soft. Add the garlic and fry until just beginning to colour. Add the puréed tomato and the reserved tomato pieces to the pan. Bring to the boil, then simmer over medium–low heat for 10 minutes. Stir in the herbs and season with salt and pepper. Simmer for 1 minute, then remove from the heat.

3 Cook the pasta in plenty of boiling salted water, until tender but still firm to the bite. Drain and transfer to a warmed serving dish. Briefly reheat the sauce. Pour over the pasta, add the basil and toss well to mix. Sprinkle with the Parmesan cheese and serve at once.

penne in a creamy mushroom sauce

ingredients

serves 4

55 g/2 oz butter
1 tbsp olive oil
6 shallots, sliced
450 g/1 lb chestnut
    mushrooms, sliced
salt and pepper
1 tsp plain flour
150 ml/5 fl oz double cream
2 tbsp port
115 g/4 oz sun-dried tomatoes
    in oil, drained and chopped
pinch freshly grated nutmeg
350 g/12 oz dried penne
2 tbsp chopped fresh flat-leaf
    parsley

method

1 Melt the butter with the olive oil in a large, heavy-based frying pan. Add the shallots and cook over low heat, stirring occasionally, for 4–5 minutes, or until softened. Add the mushrooms and cook over low heat for a further 2 minutes. Season with salt and pepper, sprinkle in the flour and cook, stirring, for 1 minute.

2 Remove the pan from the heat and gradually stir in the cream and port. Return to the heat, add the sun-dried tomatoes and grated nutmeg and cook over low heat, stirring occasionally, for 8 minutes.

3 Meanwhile, bring a large, heavy-based saucepan of lightly salted water to the boil. Add the pasta, return to the boil and cook for 8–10 minutes, or until tender but still firm to the bite. Drain the pasta well and add to the mushroom sauce. Cook for 3 minutes, then transfer to a warmed serving dish. Sprinkle with the chopped parsley and serve immediately.

fusilli with gorgonzola & mushroom sauce

ingredients

serves 4

350 g/12 oz dried fusilli
3 tbsp olive oil
350 g/12 oz wild mushrooms
    or white mushrooms, sliced
1 garlic clove, finely chopped
400 ml/14 fl oz double cream
250 g/9 oz Gorgonzola cheese,
    crumbled
salt and pepper
2 tbsp chopped fresh flat-leaf
    parsley, to garnish

method

1 Bring a large saucepan of lightly salted water to the boil. Add the pasta, return to the boil and cook for 8–10 minutes, or until tender but still firm to the bite.

2 Meanwhile, heat the olive oil in a heavy-based saucepan. Add the mushrooms and cook over low heat, stirring frequently, for 5 minutes. Add the garlic to the pan and cook for a further 2 minutes.

3 Add the cream, bring to the boil and cook for 1 minute, until slightly thickened. Stir in the cheese and cook over low heat until it has melted. Do not allow the sauce to boil once the cheese has been added. Season with salt and pepper and remove the pan from the heat.

4 Drain the pasta and tip it into the sauce. Toss well to coat, then serve immediately, garnished with the parsley.

tagliatelle with roasted artichokes & horseradish-herb sauce

ingredients

serves 2

100 g/3½ oz canned artichokes, cut into quarters

vegetable oil spray

50 g/1¾ oz fresh baby spinach leaves

100 g/3½ oz dried tagliatelle

100 ml/3½ fl oz white sauce (see page 144)

2 tsp chopped fresh basil, plus extra to garnish

1 tsp finely chopped fresh lemon thyme, plus extra to garnish

1 tsp creamed horseradish

2 tsp soured cream

method

1 Spread the artichokes out on a non-stick baking sheet, spray lightly with oil and roast in a preheated oven, 220°C/425°F/Gas Mark 7, for 20 minutes until golden brown.

2 Meanwhile, heat a large, lidded saucepan over medium heat. Add the spinach, cover and steam for 2 minutes. Remove from the heat and drain the spinach in a colander.

3 Cook the pasta according to the instructions on the packet and drain.

4 Return the drained spinach to the pan. Make the white sauce and keep warm. Add the herbs, horseradish, soured cream and artichokes and stir in the warm pasta. Heat to warm through, then serve garnished with extra herbs.

conchiglie with marinated artichoke, onion & tomato sauce

ingredients

serves 4

280 g/10 oz bottled marinated
    artichoke hearts
3 tbsp olive oil
1 onion, chopped finely
3 garlic cloves, minced
1 tsp dried oregano
¼ tsp dried chilli flakes
400 g/14 oz canned chopped
    tomatoes
salt and pepper
350 g/12 oz dried conchiglie
4 tsp freshly grated Parmesan
    cheese
3 tbsp chopped fresh flat-leaf
    parsley

method

1 Drain the artichoke hearts, reserving the marinade.
  Heat the oil in a large saucepan over medium heat.
  Add the onion and fry for 5 minutes until translucent.
  Add the garlic, oregano, chilli flakes and the reserved
  artichoke marinade. Cook for a further 5 minutes.

2 Stir in the tomatoes. Bring to the boil, then simmer over
  medium–low heat for 30 minutes. Season generously
  with salt and pepper.

3 Cook the pasta in plenty of boiling salted water until
  tender but still firm to the bite. Drain and transfer to
  a warmed serving dish.

4 Add the artichokes, Parmesan cheese and parsley
  to the sauce. Cook for a few minutes until heated
  through. Pour the sauce over the pasta, toss well
  to mix and serve at once.

fusilli with courgettes, lemon & rosemary sauce

ingredients

serves 4

6 tbsp olive oil
1 small onion, sliced very thinly
2 garlic cloves, chopped very finely
2 tbsp chopped fresh rosemary
1 tbsp chopped fresh flat-leaf
    parsley
450 g/1 lb small courgettes,
    cut into 5-mm x 4-cm/
    ¼-inch x 1½-inch strips
finely grated rind of 1 lemon
salt and pepper
450 g/1 lb fusilli tricolore
4 tbsp freshly grated Parmesan
    cheese

method

1 Heat the olive oil in a large frying pan over medium–low heat. Add the onion and gently fry, stirring occasionally, for about 10 minutes until golden.

2 Raise the heat to medium–high. Add the garlic, rosemary and parsley and cook for a few seconds, stirring. Add the courgettes and lemon rind. Cook for 5–7 minutes, stirring occasionally, until the courgettes are just tender. Season with salt and pepper. Remove from the heat.

3 Cook the pasta in plenty of boiling salted water until tender but still firm to the bite. Drain and transfer to a warmed serving dish.

4 Briefly reheat the courgettes. Pour over the pasta and toss well to mix. Sprinkle with the Parmesan cheese and serve immediately.

tagliatelle with walnuts

ingredients

serves 4

25 g/1 oz fresh white breadcrumbs
350 g/12 oz walnut pieces
2 garlic cloves, finely chopped
4 tbsp milk
4 tbsp olive oil
85 g/3 oz cream cheese
150 ml/5 fl oz single cream
salt and pepper
350 g/12 oz dried tagliatelle

method

1 Place the breadcrumbs, walnuts, garlic, milk, olive oil and cream cheese in a large mortar and grind to a smooth paste with a pestle. Alternatively, place the ingredients in a food processor and process until smooth. Stir in the cream to give a thick sauce consistency and season with salt and pepper. Set aside.

2 Bring a large heavy-based saucepan of lightly salted water to the boil. Add the pasta, return to the boil and cook for 8–10 minutes, or until tender but still firm to the bite.

3 Drain the pasta and transfer to a warmed serving dish. Add the walnut sauce and toss thoroughly to coat. Serve immediately.

tagliatelle with wild mushrooms & mascarpone

ingredients

serves 4

450 g/1 lb dried tagliatelle
55 g/2 oz butter
1 garlic clove, crushed
225 g/8 oz mixed wild
    mushrooms, sliced
250 g/9 oz mascarpone cheese
2 tbsp milk
1 tsp chopped fresh sage, plus
    extra leaves to garnish
salt and pepper
 freshly grated Parmesan
    cheese, to serve

method

1 Bring a large, heavy-based saucepan of lightly salted water to the boil. Add the pasta, return to the boil and cook for 8–10 minutes, or until tender but still firm to the bite.

2 Meanwhile, melt the butter in a separate large saucepan. Add the garlic and mushrooms and cook for 3–4 minutes.

3 Reduce the heat and stir in the mascarpone cheese, milk and sage. Season to taste with salt and pepper.

4 Drain the pasta thoroughly and add to the mushroom sauce. Toss until the pasta is well coated with the sauce. Transfer to warmed serving dishes, garnish with sage leaves and serve immediately with Parmesan cheese.

ziti with rocket

ingredients

serves 4

350 g/12 oz dried ziti, broken into
    4-cm/1½-inch lengths
5 tbsp extra-virgin olive oil
2 garlic cloves, lightly crushed
200 g/7 oz rocket
2 fresh red chillies, thickly sliced
fresh red chilli flowers, to garnish
freshly grated romano cheese,
    to serve

method

1 Bring a large, heavy-based saucepan of lightly salted water to the boil. Add the pasta, return to the boil and cook for 8–10 minutes, or until tender but still firm to the bite.

2 Meanwhile, heat the olive oil in a large, heavy-based frying pan. Add the garlic, rocket and chillies and stir-fry for 5 minutes, or until the rocket has wilted.

3 Stir 2 tablespoons of the pasta cooking water into the rocket, then drain the pasta and add to the frying pan. Cook, stirring frequently, for 2 minutes, then transfer to a warmed serving dish. Remove and discard the garlic cloves and chillies, garnish with red chilli flowers and serve immediately with the romano cheese.

variation

For a subtler, less peppery taste, replace the rocket with 200 g/7 oz baby spinach instead.

linguine with roasted garlic & red pepper sauce

ingredients

serves 4

6 large garlic cloves, unpeeled
400 g/14 oz bottled roasted red
    peppers, strained and sliced
200 g/7 oz canned chopped
    tomatoes
3 tbsp olive oil
¼ tsp dried chilli flakes
1 tsp chopped fresh thyme
    or oregano
salt and pepper
350 g/12 oz dried linguine,
    spaghetti or bucatini
freshly grated Parmesan cheese,
    to serve

method

1 Place the unpeeled garlic cloves in a shallow, ovenproof dish. Roast in a preheated oven, 200°C/400°F/Gas Mark 6, for 7–10 minutes until the cloves feel soft.

2 Put the peppers, tomatoes and oil in a food processor or blender, then purée. Squeeze the garlic flesh into the purée. Add the chilli flakes and thyme. Season with salt and pepper. Blend again, then scrape into a saucepan and set aside.

3 Cook the pasta in plenty of boiling salted water until tender but still firm to the bite. Drain and transfer to a warmed serving dish.

4 Reheat the sauce and pour over the pasta. Toss well to mix. Serve at once with Parmesan cheese.

vegetable ravioli

ingredients

serves 4

2 large aubergines, cut into
  2.5-cm/1-inch chunks
salt
6 large tomatoes
125 ml/4 fl oz olive oil
3 garlic cloves, chopped
1 large onion, chopped
3 large courgettes cut into
  2.5-cm/1-inch chunks
1 large green pepper and 1 large
  red pepper, deseeded and cut
  into 2.5-cm/1-inch chunks
4½ tsp tomato purée
½ tsp chopped fresh basil, plus
  extra sprigs to garnish
salt and pepper
basic pasta dough (see page 14)
plain flour, for dusting
6 tbsp butter
150 ml/5 fl oz single cream
85 g/3 oz freshly grated
  Parmesan cheese

method

1 To make the filling, place the aubergine pieces in a colander, sprinkle with salt and leave for 20 minutes. Rinse and drain, then pat dry on kitchen paper.

2 Blanch the tomatoes in boiling water for 2 minutes. Drain, peel and chop the flesh. Heat the oil in a large pan over a low heat. Add the garlic and onion and cook for 3 minutes. Stir in the aubergines, courgettes, tomatoes, peppers, tomato purée and chopped basil. Season to taste. Cover and simmer for 20 minutes.

3 Roll out the pasta dough on a lightly floured surface to a rectangle 2–3 mm/¹⁄₁₆–⅛ inch thick. Using a 5-cm/2-inch plain biscuit cutter, stamp out rounds.

4 Place small mounds, about 1 teaspoon each, of the filling on half of the rounds. Brush the edges with a little water, then cover with the remaining rounds, pressing the edges to seal. Place on a floured tea towel and leave to stand for 1 hour. Preheat the oven to 200°C/400°F/Gas Mark 6. Bring a large pan of lightly salted water to the boil over a medium heat. Add the ravioli and cook for about 3–4 minutes. Drain and transfer to a greased ovenproof dish, dotting each layer with butter. Pour over the cream and sprinkle over the Parmesan. Bake in the preheated oven for 20 minutes. Garnish with basil and serve.

garlic mushroom ravioli

ingredients

serves 4

75 g/2¾ oz butter
50 g/1¾ oz shallots, finely chopped
3 garlic cloves, crushed
50 g/1¾ oz mushrooms, wiped and finely chopped
½ celery stick, finely chopped
25 g/1 oz pecorino cheese, finely grated, plus extra to garnish
salt and pepper
100 g/4 oz basic pasta dough (see page 14)
plain flour, for dusting
1 egg, lightly beaten

method

1 Heat 25 g/1 oz of the butter in a frying pan. Add the shallots, 1 crushed garlic clove, the mushrooms and celery and cook for 4–5 minutes. Remove the frying pan from the heat, stir in the pecorino cheese and season to taste. Divide the pasta dough in half and wrap 1 piece in clingfilm.

2 Roll out the other piece on a lightly floured surface to a rectangle 2–3 mm/¹⁄₁₆–⅛ inch thick. Cover with a damp tea towel and roll out the other piece of dough to the same size. Place small mounds, about 1 teaspoon each, of the filling in rows 4 cm/1½ inches apart on a sheet of pasta dough. Brush the spaces between the mounds with the beaten egg. Lift the second sheet of dough on top of the first and press down firmly between the pockets of filling, pushing out any air bubbles. Using a pasta wheel or sharp knife, cut into squares. Place on a floured tea towel and leave to stand for 1 hour. Bring a heavy-based saucepan of water to the boil, add the ravioli and cook in batches for 2–3 minutes.

3 Remove with a slotted spoon and drain. Meanwhile, melt the remaining butter in a frying pan. Add the remaining garlic and plenty of pepper and cook for 1–2 minutes. Transfer ravioli to plates and pour over the garlic butter. Garnish with pecorino cheese and serve immediately.

spinach & ricotta ravioli

ingredients

serves 4

spinach pasta dough
225 g/8 oz spinach leaves
200 g/7 oz plain flour, plus extra
    for dusting
pinch of salt
2 eggs, lightly beaten
1 tbsp olive oil

filling
350 g/12 oz spinach leaves,
    coarse stalks removed
225 g/8 oz ricotta cheese
55 g/2 oz freshly grated Parmesan
    cheese, plus extra, to serve
2 eggs, lightly beaten
pinch of freshly grated nutmeg
pepper
plain flour, for dusting

method

1 To make the pasta dough, blanch the spinach in boiling water for 1 minute. Drain thoroughly and chop finely. Sift the flour into a food processor. Add the spinach, salt, eggs and olive oil and process until the dough begins to come together. Knead on a lightly floured board until smooth. Cover and let rest for 30 minutes.

2 To make the filling, cook the spinach, with just the water clinging to the leaves after washing, over low heat for 5 minutes, or until wilted. Drain and squeeze out as much moisture as possible. Cool, then chop finely. Beat the ricotta cheese until smooth, then stir in the spinach, Parmesan cheese and half the egg and season with nutmeg and pepper.

3 Halve the pasta dough. Roll out one half on a floured board. Cover, and roll out the other half. Put small mounds of filling in rows 4 cm/1½ inches apart on one sheet of dough and brush in between with the remaining egg. Cover with the other half. Press down between the mounds, pushing out any air. Cut into squares and let rest on a tea towel for 1 hour.

4 Bring a large saucepan of salted water to the boil, add the ravioli, in batches, return to the boil and cook for 5 minutes. Remove with a slotted spoon and drain on kitchen paper. Serve with grated Parmesan cheese.

al forno

lasagna

ingredients

serves 4

3 tbsp olive oil
1 onion, finely chopped
1 celery stalk, finely chopped
1 carrot, finely chopped
100 g/3½ oz pancetta or rindless
    lean bacon, finely chopped
175 g/6 oz minced beef
175 g/6 oz minced pork
50 ml/2 fl oz dry red wine
150 ml/5 fl oz beef stock
1 tbsp tomato purée
salt and pepper
1 clove
1 bay leaf
150 ml/5 fl oz boiling milk
4 tbsp unsalted butter, diced,
    plus extra for greasing
400 g/14 oz dried lasagna
béchamel sauce (see below)
140 g/5 oz mozzarella cheese
140 g/5 oz Parmesan cheese

basic béchamel sauce

25g/1 oz butter
1 tbsp plain flour
350 ml (12 fl oz) warm milk
salt and pepper

method

1 Heat the olive oil in a large, heavy-based saucepan. Add the onion, celery, carrot, pancetta, beef and pork and cook over medium heat, stirring frequently for 10 minutes, or until lightly browned.

2 Add the wine, stock and tomato purée to the pan, boil and reduce. Season with salt and pepper, add the clove and bay leaf and pour in the milk. Cover and simmer over low heat for 1½ hours. Remove from the heat and discard the clove and bay leaf.

3 To make the béchamel sauce, melt the butter in a pan over the low heat. Add the flour and stir with a wooden spoon. Turn the heat up a little and continue stirring for 2 minutes. Add half of the milk and stir until you have a smooth paste. Add the remaining milk, stirring until you have a smooth, white sauce. Season.

4 Lightly grease a large, ovenproof dish with butter. Place a layer of lasagna in the bottom and cover it with a layer of meat sauce. Spoon a layer of béchamel sauce on top and sprinkle with one third of the cheese. Make layers until all the ingredients are used, ending with a topping of béchamel sauce and sprinkled cheese.

5 Dot the top of the lasagna with the diced butter and bake in a preheated oven, 200°C/400°F/Gas Mark 6, for 30 minutes, or until golden and bubbling.

marsala mushroom lasagna

ingredients

serves 4

exotic mushroom sauce

2 tbsp olive oil

2 garlic cloves, crushed

1 large onion, finely chopped

225 g/8 oz mushrooms, sliced

300 g/10½ oz fresh minced chicken

85 g/3 oz chicken livers, finely chopped

115 g/4 oz prosciutto, diced

150 ml/5 fl oz Marsala wine

285 g/10 oz canned chopped tomatoes

1 tbsp chopped fresh basil leaves

2 tbsp tomato purée

salt and pepper

béchamel sauce (see page 176)

butter, for greasing

14 sheets dried no-precook lasagna

85 g/3 oz grated Parmesan cheese

method

1 To make the mushroom sauce, heat the olive oil in a large, heavy-based saucepan. Add the garlic, onion and mushrooms and cook, stirring frequently, for 6 minutes. Add the minced chicken, chicken livers and prosciutto and cook over low heat for 12 minutes, or until the meat has browned.

2 Stir the Marsala, tomatoes, basil and tomato purée into the mixture, and cook for 4 minutes. Season with salt and pepper, cover and simmer for 30 minutes. Uncover, then simmer for a further 15 minutes.

3 Make a triple quantity of béchamel sauce.

4 Lightly grease an ovenproof dish with butter. Arrange sheets of lasagna over the base of the dish, spoon over a layer of the exotic mushroom sauce, then spoon over a layer of béchamel sauce. Place another layer of lasagna on top and repeat the process twice, finishing with a layer of béchamel sauce. Sprinkle over the grated cheese and bake in a preheated oven, 190°C/375°F/Gas Mark 5, for 35 minutes, or until golden brown and bubbling. Serve immediately.

pasticcio

ingredients

serves 4

1 tbsp olive oil
1 onion, chopped
2 garlic cloves, finely chopped
450 g/1 lb fresh minced lamb
2 tbsp tomato purée
2 tbsp plain flour
300 ml/10 fl oz chicken stock
salt and pepper
1 tsp ground cinnamon
115 g/4 oz dried short-cut
    macaroni
2 beefsteak tomatoes, sliced
300 ml/10 fl oz Greek-style yogurt
2 eggs, lightly beaten

method

1 Heat the olive oil in a large heavy-based frying pan. Add the onion and garlic and cook over low heat, stirring occasionally, for 5 minutes, or until softened. Add the lamb and cook, breaking it up with a wooden spoon, until browned all over. Add the tomato purée and sprinkle in the flour. Cook, stirring, for 1 minute, then stir in the chicken stock. Season with salt and pepper and stir in the cinnamon. Bring to the boil, reduce the heat, cover and cook for 25 minutes.

2 Meanwhile, bring a large heavy-based saucepan of lightly salted water to the boil. Add the pasta, return to the boil and cook for 8–10 minutes, or until tender but still firm to the bite.

3 Spoon the lamb mixture into a large ovenproof dish and arrange the tomato slices on top. Drain the pasta and transfer to a bowl. Add the yogurt and eggs and mix well. Spoon the pasta mixture on top of the lamb and bake in a preheated oven, 190°C/375°F/Gas Mark 5, for 1 hour. Serve immediately.

cannelloni with ham & ricotta

ingredients

serves 4

2 tbsp olive oil
2 onions, chopped
2 garlic cloves, finely chopped
1 tbsp shredded fresh basil
800 g/1 lb 12 oz chopped
    tomatoes
1 tbsp tomato purée
salt and pepper
350 g/12 oz dried cannelloni tubes
butter, for greasing
225 g/8 oz ricotta cheese
115 g/4 oz cooked ham, diced
1 egg
55 g/2 oz freshly grated
    romano cheese

method

1 Heat the olive oil in a large, heavy-based frying pan.
   Add the onions and garlic and cook over low heat,
   stirring occasionally, for 5 minutes, or until the onion
   is softened. Add the basil, chopped tomatoes and their
   can juices and tomato purée and season with salt and
   pepper. Reduce the heat and simmer for 30 minutes,
   or until thickened.

2 Meanwhile, bring a large, heavy-based saucepan of
   lightly salted water to the boil. Add the dried cannelloni
   tubes, return to the boil and cook for 8–10 minutes,
   or until tender but still firm to the bite. Using a slotted
   spoon, transfer the cannelloni tubes to a large plate
   and pat dry with kitchen paper.

3 Grease a large, shallow ovenproof dish with butter.
   Mix the ricotta, ham and egg together in a bowl and
   season with salt and pepper. Using a teaspoon, fill
   the cannelloni tubes with the ricotta, ham and egg
   mixture and place in a single layer in the dish. Pour
   the tomato sauce over the cannelloni and sprinkle
   with the grated romano cheese. Bake in a preheated
   oven, 180°C/350°F/Gas Mark 4, for 30 minutes, or until
   golden brown. Serve at once.

chicken lasagna

ingredients

serves 6

2 tbsp olive oil
900 g/2 lb fresh minced chicken
1 garlic clove, finely chopped
4 carrots, chopped
4 leeks, sliced
450 ml/16 fl oz chicken stock
2 tbsp tomato purée
salt and pepper
béchamel sauce (see page 176)
115 g/4 oz Cheddar cheese, grated
1 tsp Dijon mustard
115 g/4 oz dried no-precook
    lasagna

method

1 Heat the oil in a heavy-based saucepan. Add the chicken and cook over medium heat, breaking it up with a wooden spoon, for 5 minutes, or until it is browned all over. Add the garlic, carrots and leeks to the pan and cook, stirring occasionally, for 5 minutes.

2 Stir in the chicken stock and tomato purée and season with salt and pepper. Bring to the boil, reduce the heat, cover and simmer for 30 minutes.

3 Make a double quantity of béchamel sauce.

4 Whisk half the cheese and the mustard into the hot béchamel sauce. In a large ovenproof dish, make alternate layers of the chicken mixture, lasagna and cheese sauce, ending with a layer of cheese sauce. Sprinkle with the remaining cheese and bake in a preheated oven, 190°C/375°F/Gas Mark 5, for 1 hour, or until golden brown and bubbling. Serve at once.

chicken & wild mushroom cannelloni

ingredients

serves 4

butter, for greasing
2 tbsp olive oil
2 garlic cloves, crushed
1 large onion, finely chopped
225 g/8 oz wild mushrooms, sliced
350 g/12 oz minced chicken
115 g/4 oz prosciutto, diced
150 ml/5 fl oz Marsala wine
200 g/7 oz canned chopped
  tomatoes
1 tbsp shredded fresh basil leaves
2 tbsp tomato purée
salt and pepper
10–12 dried cannelloni tubes
béchamel sauce (see page 176)
85 g/3 oz freshly grated Parmesan
  cheese

method

1 Lightly grease a large ovenproof dish. Heat the olive oil in a heavy-based frying pan. Add the garlic, onion and mushrooms and cook over low heat, stirring frequently, for 8–10 minutes. Add the minced chicken and prosciutto and cook, stirring frequently, until browned all over. Stir in the Marsala, tomatoes and their can juices, basil and tomato purée and cook for 4 minutes. Season with salt and pepper, then cover and simmer for 30 minutes. Uncover, stir and simmer for 15 minutes.

2 Meanwhile, bring a large, heavy-based saucepan of lightly salted water to the boil. Add the pasta, return to the boil and cook for 8–10 minutes, or until tender but still firm to the bite. Using a slotted spoon, transfer the pasta to a plate and pat dry with kitchen paper.

3 Make a double quantity of béchamel sauce.

4 Fill the cannelloni tubes with the chicken, prosciutto and mushroom mixture. Transfer them to the ovenproof dish. Pour the béchamel sauce over them to cover completely and sprinkle with the grated Parmesan cheese. Bake the cannelloni in a preheated oven, 190°C/375°F/Gas Mark 5, for 30 minutes, or until golden brown and bubbling. Serve at once.

lasagna alla marinara

ingredients

serves 6

1 tbsp butter

225 g/8 oz raw prawns, shelled, deveined and coarsely chopped

450 g/1 lb monkfish fillets, skinned and chopped

225 g/8 oz chestnut mushrooms, chopped

béchamel sauce (see page 176)

salt and pepper

400 g/14 oz canned chopped tomatoes

1 tbsp chopped fresh chervil

1 tbsp shredded fresh basil

175 g/6 oz dried no-precook lasagna

85 g/3 oz freshly grated Parmesan cheese

method

1 Melt the butter in a large, heavy-based saucepan. Add the prawns and monkfish and cook over medium heat for 3–5 minutes, or until the prawns change colour. Transfer the prawns to a small heatproof bowl with a slotted spoon. Add the mushrooms to the pan and cook, stirring occasionally, for 5 minutes. Transfer the fish and mushrooms to the bowl.

2 Make a triple quantity of béchamel sauce.

3 Stir the fish mixture, with any juices, into the béchamel sauce and season to taste with salt and pepper.

4 Layer the tomatoes, chervil, basil, fish mixture and lasagna sheets in a large ovenproof dish, ending with a layer of the fish mixture. Sprinkle evenly with the grated Parmesan cheese. Bake in a preheated oven, 190°C/375°F/Gas Mark 5, for 35 minutes, or until golden brown, then serve immediately.

baked tuna & ricotta rigatoni

ingredients

serves 4

450 g/1 lb dried rigatoni
115 g/4 oz sun-dried tomatoes
in oil, drained and sliced

filling

200 g/7 oz canned flaked tuna,
drained
225 g/8 oz ricotta cheese

sauce

125 ml/4 fl oz double cream
225 g/8 oz freshly grated
Parmesan cheese
salt and pepper

method

1 Lightly grease a large ovenproof dish with butter. Bring
a large, heavy-based saucepan of lightly salted water to
the boil. Add the rigatoni, return to the boil and cook
for 8–10 minutes, or until just tender but still firm to
the bite. Drain the pasta and let stand until cool
enough to handle.

2 Meanwhile, mix the tuna and ricotta cheese together
in a bowl to form a soft paste. Spoon the mixture into
a pastry bag and use to fill the rigatoni. Arrange the
filled pasta tubes side by side in the prepared dish.

3 To make the sauce, mix the cream and Parmesan
cheese together in a bowl and season with salt and
pepper. Spoon the sauce over the rigatoni and top
with the sun-dried tomatoes, arranged in a criss-cross
pattern. Bake in a preheated oven, 200°C/400°F/Gas
Mark 6, for 20 minutes. Serve hot straight from the dish.

layered spaghetti with smoked salmon & prawns

ingredients

serves 6

350 g/12 oz dried spaghetti
70 g/2½ oz butter, plus extra
    for greasing
béchamel sauce (see page 176)
200 g/7 oz smoked salmon,
    cut into strips
280 g/10 oz jumbo prawns,
    cooked, shelled and deveined
115 g/4 oz freshly grated Parmesan
    cheese

method

1 Bring a large saucepan of lightly salted water to the boil. Add the pasta, return to the boil and cook for 8–10 minutes, or until tender but still firm to the bite. Drain well, return to the pan, add 4 tablespoons of the butter and toss well.

2 Make a double quantity of béchamel sauce.

3 Spoon half the spaghetti into a large, greased ovenproof dish, cover with the strips of smoked salmon, then top with the prawns. Pour over half the béchamel sauce and sprinkle with half the Parmesan. Add the remaining spaghetti, cover with the remaining sauce and sprinkle with the remaining Parmesan. Dice the remaining butter and dot it over the surface.

4 Bake in a preheated oven, 180°C/350°F/Gas Mark 4, for 15 minutes, or until the top is golden brown. Serve immediately.

macaroni cheese

ingredients

serves 4

225 g/8 oz macaroni
béchamel sauce (see page 176)
1 egg, beaten
125 g/4½ oz mature Cheddar
   cheese, grated
1 tbsp wholegrain mustard
2 tbsp chopped fresh chives
salt and pepper
4 tomatoes, sliced
125 g/4½ oz Red Leicester cheese,
   grated
60 g/2¼ oz blue cheese, grated
2 tbsp sunflower seeds
snipped fresh chives, to garnish

method

1 Bring a large saucepan of lightly salted water to the boil and cook the macaroni for 8–10 minutes, or until just tender. Drain well and place in an ovenproof dish.

2 Make a double quantity of béchamel sauce.

3 Stir the beaten egg, Cheddar cheese, mustard and chives into the béchamel sauce and season with salt and pepper. Spoon the mixture over the macaroni, making sure it is well covered. Top with a layer of the sliced tomatoes.

4 Sprinkle over the Red Leicester cheese, blue cheese and sunflower seeds. Place on a baking sheet and bake in a preheated oven, 190°C/375°F/Gas Mark 5, for 25–30 minutes, or until bubbling and golden. Garnish with snipped fresh chives and serve at once.

double cheese macaroni

ingredients

serves 4

225 g/8 oz dried macaroni
250 g/9 oz ricotta cheese
1½ tbsp wholegrain mustard
3 tbsp snipped fresh chives,
    plus extra to garnish
salt and pepper
200 g/7 oz cherry tomatoes,
    halved
100 g/3½ oz sun-dried tomatoes
    in oil, drained and chopped
butter or oil, for greasing
100 g/3½ oz Cheddar cheese,
    grated

method

1 Bring a saucepan of lightly salted water to the boil.

2 Add the pasta and cook for 10–12 minutes, or until tender. Drain. Mix the ricotta with the mustard, chives and salt and pepper.

3 Stir in the macaroni, cherry tomatoes and sun-dried tomatoes. Grease a 1.7-litre/3-pint ovenproof dish, spoon in the macaroni mixture and sprinkle with the cheese. Then bake in a preheated oven, 190°C/375°F/ Gas Mark 5, for 20 minutes or until the top is golden.

vegetarian lasagna

ingredients

serves 4

béchamel sauce (see page 176)

olive oil, for brushing

2 aubergines, sliced

2 tbsp butter

1 garlic clove, finely chopped

4 courgettes, sliced

1 tbsp finely chopped fresh
flat-leaf parsley

1 tbsp finely chopped fresh
marjoram

225 g/8 oz mozzarella cheese,
grated

625 ml/20 fl oz strained canned
tomatoes

175 g/6 oz dried no-precook
lasagna

salt and pepper

55 g/2 oz freshly grated Parmesan
cheese

method

1 Make a single quantity of béchamel sauce.

2 Brush a griddle pan with olive oil and heat until
smoking. Add half the aubergine slices and cook over
medium heat for 8 minutes, or until golden brown
all over. Remove from the griddle pan and drain on
kitchen paper. Repeat with the remaining slices.

3 Melt the butter in a frying pan and add the garlic,
courgettes, parsley and marjoram. Cook over medium
heat, stirring frequently, for 5 minutes, or until the
courgettes are golden all over. Remove and drain
on kitchen paper.

4 Layer the aubergine, courgettes, mozzarella, strained
tomatoes and lasagna in an ovenproof dish brushed
with olive oil, seasoning as you go and finishing with
a layer of lasagna. Pour over the béchamel sauce,
sprinkle with the Parmesan cheese and bake in a
preheated oven, 200°C/400°F/Gas Mark 6, for 30–40
minutes, or until golden brown. Serve at once.

mixed vegetable agnolotti

ingredients

serves 4

pasta dough

200 g/7 oz white bread flour
1 tsp salt
1 tbsp olive oil
2 eggs, lightly beaten

filling

125 ml/4 fl oz olive oil
1 red onion, chopped
3 garlic cloves, chopped
2 large aubergines, cut into chunks
3 large courgettes, cut into chunks
6 beefsteak tomatoes, peeled,
    deseeded and chopped
1 large green pepper, deseeded
    and diced
1 large red pepper, deseeded
    and diced
1 tbsp sun-dried tomato purée
1 tbsp shredded fresh basil
salt and pepper

butter, for greasing
plain flour, for dusting
85 g/3 oz freshly grated
    Parmesan cheese
mixed salad leaves, to serve

method

1 To make the pasta dough, sift the flour into a food
processor. Add the salt, eggs and olive oil and process
until the dough begins to come together. Knead on a
lightly floured board until smooth. Cover and let rest for
30 minutes.

2 To make the filling, heat the olive oil in a large,
heavy-based saucepan. Add the onion and garlic and
cook over low heat, stirring occasionally, for 5 minutes,
or until softened. Add the aubergine, courgettes,
tomatoes, green and red peppers, sun-dried tomato
purée and basil. Season with salt and pepper, cover
and simmer gently, stirring occasionally, for 20 minutes.

3 Lightly grease an ovenproof dish with butter. Roll out
the pasta dough on a lightly floured board and stamp
out 7.5-cm/3-inch circles with a plain cutter. Place a
spoonful of the vegetable filling on one side of each
circle. Dampen the edges slightly and fold the pasta
circles over, pressing together to seal.

4 Bring a large pan of lightly salted water to the boil.
Add the agnolotti, return to the boil and cook for
3–4 minutes. Remove with a slotted spoon, drain and
transfer to the dish. Sprinkle with the Parmesan and
bake in a preheated oven, 200°C/400°F/Gas Mark 6,
Serve with salad leaves.

baked pasta with mushrooms

ingredients

serves 4

140 g/5 oz fontina cheese, thinly sliced

béchamel sauce (see page 176)

6 tbsp butter, plus extra for greasing

350 g/12 oz mixed wild mushrooms, sliced

350 g/12 oz dried tagliatelle

2 egg yolks

salt and pepper

4 tbsp freshly grated romano cheese

mixed salad leaves, to serve

method

1 Make a double quantity of béchamel sauce. Stir the fontina cheese into the béchamel sauce and set aside.

2 Melt 2 tablespoons of the butter in a large saucepan. Add the mushrooms and cook over low heat, stirring occasionally, for 10 minutes.

3 Meanwhile, bring a large saucepan of lightly salted water to the boil. Add the pasta, return to the boil and cook for 8–10 minutes, or until tender but still firm to the bite. Drain, return to the pan and add the remaining butter, the egg yolks and about one third of the sauce, then season with salt and pepper. Toss well to mix, then gently stir in the mushrooms.

4 Lightly grease a large, ovenproof dish with butter and spoon in the pasta mixture. Pour over the remaining sauce evenly and sprinkle with the grated romano cheese. Bake in a preheated oven, 200°C/400°F/Gas Mark 6, for 15–20 minutes, or until golden brown. Serve immediately with mixed salad leaves.

mushroom cannelloni

ingredients

serves 4

12 dried cannelloni tubes
2 tbsp butter
450 g/1 lb mixed wild mushrooms,
    finely chopped
1 garlic clove, finely chopped
85 g/3 oz fresh breadcrumbs
150 ml/5 fl oz milk
4 tbsp olive oil, plus extra
    for brushing
225 g/8 oz ricotta cheese
6 tbsp freshly grated Parmesan
    cheese
salt and pepper
2 tbsp pine nuts
2 tbsp slivered almonds

tomato sauce

2 tbsp olive oil
1 onion, finely chopped
1 garlic clove, finely chopped
800 g/1 lb 12 oz canned chopped
    tomatoes
1 tbsp tomato purée
8 black olives, pitted and chopped
salt and pepper

method

1 Bring a large saucepan of lightly salted water to the
boil. Add the cannelloni tubes, return to the boil and
cook for 8–10 minutes, or until tender but still firm to
the bite. Drain, transfer the tubes to a plate and pat dry.

2 Meanwhile, make the tomato sauce. Heat the olive oil
in a frying pan. Add the onion and garlic and cook over
low heat for 5 minutes, or until softened. Add the
tomatoes and their can juices, tomato purée and olives
and season with salt and pepper. Bring to the boil and
cook for 3–4 minutes. Pour the sauce into an large
ovenproof dish brushed with olive oil.

3 To make the filling, melt the butter in a heavy-based
frying pan. Add the mushrooms and garlic and cook
over medium heat, stirring frequently, for 3–5 minutes,
or until tender. Remove the frying pan from the heat.
Mix the breadcrumbs, milk and olive oil together in a
large bowl, then stir in the ricotta, mushroom mixture
and 4 tablespoons of the Parmesan cheese. Season
with salt and pepper.

4 Fill the cannelloni tubes with the mushroom mixture
and place them in the dish. Brush with olive oil and
sprinkle with the remaining Parmesan cheese, pine
nuts and almonds. Bake in a preheated oven, 190°C/
375°F/Gas Mark 5, for 25 minutes, or until golden.

cannelloni with spinach & ricotta

ingredients

serves 4

12 dried cannelloni tubes,
    7.5 cm/3 inches long
butter, for greasing

filling

140 g/5 oz cooked lean ham,
    chopped
140 g/5 oz frozen spinach,
    thawed and drained
115 g/4 oz ricotta cheese
1 egg
3 tbsp freshly grated romano
    cheese
pinch of freshly grated nutmeg
salt and pepper

cheese sauce

2 tbsp unsalted butter
2 tbsp plain flour
625 ml/20 fl oz hot milk
85 g/3 oz freshly grated Gruyère
    cheese
salt and pepper

method

1 Bring a large saucepan of lightly salted water to the boil. Add the cannelloni tubes, return to the boil and cook for 6–7 minutes, or until nearly tender. Drain, transfer the tubes to a plate and pat dry.

2 Process the ham, spinach and ricotta in a food processor for a few seconds until combined. Add the egg and romano cheese and process again to a smooth paste. Transfer to a bowl and season with nutmeg, salt and pepper.

3 Grease an ovenproof dish with butter. Spoon the filling into a pastry bag fitted with a 1-cm/ ½-inch tip. Carefully pipe the filling into the cannelloni tubes and place in the dish.

4 To make the cheese sauce, melt the butter in a saucepan. Add the flour and cook over low heat, stirring constantly, for 1 minute. Gradually stir in the hot milk then bring to the boil, stirring constantly. Simmer over the lowest possible heat, stirring frequently, for 10 minutes until thickened and smooth. Remove the pan from the heat, stir in the Gruyère cheese and season with salt and pepper.

5 Spoon the cheese sauce over the cannelloni. Cover with foil and bake in a preheated oven, 180°C/350°F/Gas Mark 4, for 20–25 minutes. Serve immediately.

index